Why Don't I Feel Better?

Why Don't I Feel Better?

HEALING THE
RECOVERING ALCOHOLIC

Joyce Bismack

BEAR & COMPANY
P U B L I S H I N G
SANTA FE, NEW MEXICO

LIBRARY OF CONGRESS CATALOGING-IN-PUBLICATION DATA
Bismack, Joyce, 1939-
    Why don't I feel better? : healing the recovering alcoholic /
Joyce Bismack.
        p. cm.
    Includes bibliographical references.
    ISBN 0-939680-77-7 (pbk.)
        1. Alcoholics—Rehabilitation—United States. 2. Alcoholism—
United States—Psychological aspects. 3. Alcoholism—Religious
aspects. 4. New age movement—United States. I. Title.
HV5279.B56 1991   90-49607
362.29'286—dc20   CIP

Bear & Company, Inc.
Santa Fe, NM 87504-2860

Cover photo: Christopher Speakman © 1991
Design & illustration: Marilyn Hager Biethan
Editing: Brandt Morgan

Printed in the United States of America by BookCrafters

9 8 7 6 5 4 3 2 1

Contents

Acknowledgments

I would like to thank Barbara Hand Clow for her support as editor. My thanks as well to Barbara Doern Drew and Brandt Morgan for their tireless patience in editing the manuscript, and to the entire staff of Bear & Company.

My appreciation goes also to the great world teachers whose inspiration created this work: the Tibetan Dwal Khul, Hilarion, Carl Jung, Roberto Assagioli, Sri Aurobindo, Abraham Maslow, and Jesus the Christ.

My thanks to Simone Beaulieu, without whose assistance this book would not have been possible, and to Tricia Long for her assistance in typing the manuscript.

I offer this book in memory of Phelps Montgomery.

Preface

I grew up in a middle-class family in the Northeast. Early in life I experienced feelings of alienation, feelings of being different. My parents' worldview and values somehow were too superficial. I remember wondering that if this was all life had to offer, then why live at all?

I knew that I had been severely traumatized early in childhood, but it wasn't until four years ago that I remembered that I had been molested by a male relative at the age of five. I had suppressed the trauma, but all the while it had been affecting my emotional and psychological development. I had developed a short-term memory problem and a tendency toward alcoholism, and I had difficulty with relationships. I finally found the courage to face the rape exactly as it was. As a child I had lacked the energy of my own inner male and ended up becoming vulnerable to this type of abuse.

My childhood was an unhappy one. I tried fitting in for a long time to no avail, and then when I was twenty-two I had a mystical experience—an expansion of consciousness that profoundly transformed my life. I had been at a mountain resort for a weekend retreat. I was facing the death of someone I loved. The death brought me a profound sadness, yet at the same time I surrendered to God's will.

This was a time of deep spiritual crisis for me, and the intense stress produced a shift in my awareness. I heard the cry of my soul, and something manifested itself from the unseen. My higher self descended and took control. From the midst of turmoil, I was suddenly lifted high above it, and all struggle ceased. I was transported in a wave of bliss. I felt like a ship peacefully and securely riding out the storm. I seemed to be merging with the mountains, the trees, and the water. They were part of me and I was part of them. We were one; there was no longer any separation. I felt a new joy in living that I had not known before.

This experience began to recur periodically, and I had no control over it. It took place in times of dire stress. It came and went quickly, leaving no trace except upon my soul. But now I see that just as the lower self can ascend and take control, as in addiction, so can the higher self descend and take control in times of spiritual crisis. These experiences were to provide a stabilizing influence throughout my life, though a period of ten years passed during which they did not occur at all.

At around age thirty my world fell apart. I had experienced a series of disappointments; my mystic vision had long since faded. Having tasted ecstasy once, it is often difficult to accept the fact that it may not return. Ecstasy had been my addiction, and I had been content to stay there, centered in myself.

Then a depression or ennui set in that was to last many years. There were no consolations of any sort. My relationships had not been working, and deep down I felt a profound dissatisfaction with life and what it had to offer. I was deeply alienated from those around me and sensed that I was not really who I thought I was. It was then that I had my first alcoholic drink. I was afraid to go on.

During that time of depression, I had a long-term relationship with an alcoholic. All my efforts to control his drinking failed, and the relationship ended in tragedy. For the first time in my life, I saw the devastating effects of alcohol on a life. His death profoundly affected me, but still

I didn't see that I had a problem. I had been a periodic drinker, but now my drinking gradually worsened. I began using alcohol to cope more and more—to drown out the emptiness I felt inside.

I had also had a lot of career difficulties, due to the fact that I didn't know who I was. I would train for a field and then lose interest in it. I had worked on several master's degree programs and not finished them. For four years I had a dreary job in an insurance company, and in 1977 I was put on probation for alcoholism. It was getting harder for me to hide the effects of my drinking. In 1978 I quit my job and opened a bookstore, then went bankrupt. In 1979 I made one of my best decisions: I moved to California. However, my addiction problem continued to get worse.

The reason for my drinking was obscured from me all those years. It was partly due to my childhood trauma. Yet I was also experiencing a spiritual crisis; I was resisting the next step.

The awareness that I had a drinking problem came slowly—not at all like a bolt of lightning. I went to Alcoholics Anonymous (AA) and found comfort there, even though I felt that their values were different from mine. In college I became an agnostic, and this period of skepticism lasted eighteen years. I could no longer relate to an external god. After a while AA stopped working for me, and I became preoccupied with why AA worked for some and not for others. I thought I could control the disease by learning all I could about it, so I took some courses on the scientific aspects of alcoholism at the local college.

In 1985 I traveled to a nearby city to take a class on the nature of the soul. This course, written by Lucille Ceder-crans, is a new thoughtform of an ancient wisdom. It took a year for me to complete. It put me in touch with my higher self, and I started having mystical experiences again. For the first time I realized that my essence is separate from my personality. This course traced human evolution from the Fall and described how humankind has gotten to where it is today. Slowly I remembered who I was and why I was here at this particular time in history. I was to give to the world a new approach to alcoholism. My life now had meaning and purpose.

Introduction

The power to create and the power to experience meaning provide us with reasons for living. Alcoholics have lost this meaning. Unless it is restored, abstinence is quite difficult to maintain. This book explores these issues, with an eye toward reestablishing health and sobriety through spiritual growth and understanding.

In the past, most therapists believed that the personality was the sum total of human nature. They had little or no awareness of the higher self and its relationship to the human personality. Even today, psychology primarily perceives the personality as existing to seek ego satisfaction; it doesn't provide answers to the deeper meaning and purpose of life. Yet many people are unconsciously seeking answers to these questions. Recognizing that the scientific worldview is not enough, many of them turn to addictions instead.

We need to have an addiction treatment program based on a solid understanding of human nature. We will not find answers in psychology alone. As spiritual master Sri Aurobindo eloquently said:

> I find it difficult to take these Western [psychologists] at all seriously. . . yet perhaps one ought to, for half-knowledge is a powerful thing and can be a great obstacle to the Truth. . . . They look from down up and explain the higher by the lower obscurities; but the foundation of these things is above and not below. . . . The significance of the lotus is not to be found by analyzing the secrets of the mud from which it grows; its secret is to be found in the heavenly archetype of the lotus that blooms forever in the light above.[1]

In other words, until we begin to know human con-sciousness, we will not understand addictions completely. Fortunately, a redefinition of self is being explored by some theorists today. The soul is being studied as the real essence that gives meaning and purpose to our lives. It is the unifying center of the personality; understanding the soul is what puts us in touch with our real power. Addiction is a person-ality problem; experiencing the soul is what eradicates our addictions.

This book explains how to differentiate between the higher self and the personality. It teaches the process of acquiring increasing awareness of the higher self, for that alone can restore the alcoholic to sanity and sobriety. Addic-tions are a kind of insanity, and even though our soul awaits contact with us, we must first create a realization of it. We have the power within us to heal ourselves.

This book presents an expanded version of the addiction process. It is for alcoholics who are seeking a deeper under-standing of addiction than they are receiving in current programs. For the most part it is addressed directly to the alcoholic; however, it is also written for loved ones of alcohol-ics and for those who believe it is possible to move beyond being a victim of alcoholism.

With this book I assure you that this is possible, although careful observation of our emotional states will always be necessary. I have personally used the techniques described here to maintain quality sobriety. In some ways this book is a distilled version of the course I put myself through. Over a period of years I have done all the exercises in one form or another. I offer it to you as a part of myself, and I suggest that you read it on whatever level feels right for you. Trust your intuition, and it will lead you to truth.

The scientific worldview is limited in how it can help us. It does not get the point of who we really are: divine beings in the process of evolving to a higher level of awareness. We are never victims of the past and are always capable of controlling our present and creating our future.

I have written this book because I know that there are more of you like me out there. You may not be fitting in with your usual groups anymore; you may be looking for freedom from conditioning patterns. You may be experiencing a sense of distance or detachment from your family or culture. You may sense that there is more to reality than the modern world believes. Perhaps you are becoming more and more dissatisfied with what you see in your external world, or perhaps self-awareness is becoming more important to you in your quest for spiritual truth. Well, hello, you are awakening! And welcome. There are more of us than you may have imagined.

In 1980 Marilyn Ferguson, in her book *The Aquarian Conspiracy*, reported that she had studied a group of people who were quietly and powerfully bringing about a social transformation. This group still exists, and though it is not formally organized, the people involved in it share a common perspective and a common vision of the world. They are helping to create a shift in consciousness more radical than the Industrial Revolution.

As Ferguson points out, the old ways are not working. Cultural values are disintegrating to make way for a "new paradigm" that will synthesize the left and right brains, the science of the West with the intuitive wisdom of the East. Humanity is on the verge of radically altering its existence. We are in the midst of another accelerated technological and scientific revolution that will have a profound impact on us individually and collectively.

At this critical time in history, as the Age of Pisces shifts into the Age of Aquarius, we notice that our perceptions of reality have changed. We are seeing a major shift in our attitudes and values and our responsibilities for the future of the planet. We feel a need to define our perceptions and experiences in a new way.

Alcohol and drug treatment programs will be affected by this paradigm shift. Operating from the premise that there is value in all of life's experiences—even addiction—new-paradigm healers are searching for new methods of healing.

Culture has a strong impact on alcoholic recovery programs; when a culture changes, its recovery programs must also change. For recovery programs to evolve into the New Age, new ideas and applications are essential. If we desire to take a leap into the new consciousness, we must be willing to let go of old attitudes that are no longer relevant to our present reality. That belief is the foundation for this book, which offers a new approach to alcoholism.

For an understanding of the influences on present-day alcohol and drug recovery programs, we need to go back and review the forces that shaped our current attitudes. In *The Death of Nature*, Carolyn Merchant documents how the rise of modern science and the economic needs of preindustrial capitalism in the sixteenth and seventeenth centuries shifted the "normative image" of the world from that of a living organism to that of a dead machine. This machine image, this view of the world composed of isolated, nonliving parts moving and interacting as separate entities, grew out of a Christian context in which divinity and spirit were divorced from matter. Modern science undermined the belief in God and spirit. This separation of nature and humanity led to the belief that humanity could control nature. The prevailing philosophy became one of humanity against nature, not one of humanity and nature working together.

This attitude has led to the destruction of much of nature. We see ourselves no longer as children of God but as flawed images of a machine with defective programming. We trust only what can be measured, counted, or acquired. Life seems empty, and this emptiness is reflected in literature and art. This philosophy, called the "mechanistic" worldview, was introduced by the philosophers Isaac Newton and René Descartes. This worldview has permeated our perceptions of the world; it has become the "American Way."

Because we can see, touch, and feel this material world, we believe it is more real than our psychological states and spiritual aspirations. This is the reason we have not made much progress in our addiction treatment programs. We have inhibited our own progress. We believe the physical world is all there is, and we limit ourselves to physical parameters.

Of course, the material world *does* exist, but it is only a part of reality—the part that has manifested in concrete, physical form. And the internal psyche, the world of ideas, our psychological and emotional states, are *determinants* of the material world. Science does not understand human nature; it does not even know how to define it. By its own definition, science only accepts as truth that which can be observed, measured, touched, and felt.

With addiction, focusing on physical cures falls into the trap of believing we are only our physical bodies. Alcoholism is usually defined as alcohol's effect on a person's physical body and exterior life. But recovery programs that focus only on physical cures fall short because they fail to take into consideration our deeper natures. This book explores our deeper natures and offers ways to tap a wellspring of spiritual power to bring about lasting sobriety and fulfillment in our lives.

ONE

Causes of Alcoholism

What does the increase in alcoholic addiction mean? At this time New Age energies are bombarding the Earth, urging us toward transformation. Addictions, particularly alcoholism, are shields against the higher energies seeking entrance to our psyches. They form a permanent barrier between us and our higher selves. Fear of change is characteristic of alcoholism.

Alcoholism is a complex problem that cannot be easily defined. What is it? Some say it is a behavioral disorder; some say it is a problem in living or a symbol of moral and ethical weakness; some say it is a neurosis, a mental obsession, or a physical allergy; and some say it is a disease. Some even say that it is just another bad habit that can be cured with will power.

There is some truth in all of these statements. However, scientists do not know the full causes of alcoholism. The problem has never been accurately defined or understood, and no one has put together all the pieces. Most researchers deal with only one aspect of alcoholism: the lower self of the addicted person. This is why many treatment programs do not work as well as they might. They focus on treating symptoms and not the disease itself.

Treatment programs based on partial truths work for

some, but without the whole truth, permanent sobriety may be difficult to maintain. Years of observation have given me a good idea of why treatment programs don't work. A true recovery program will transform us addicts into the multidimensional beings we are meant to be. Multidimensionality is the state of existing or being aware of more than one dimension at the same time. As Sri Aurobindo put it:

> You must know the whole before you can know the part and the highest before you can truly understand the lowest. That is the promise of the greater psychology awaiting its hour before which these poor groupings will disappear and come to nothing.[2]

Most "how-to" books on subjects ranging from weight control to psychological self-help seem to have a common failing: they try to give answers without really addressing the problem. Most of them stop at left-brain analysis. Metaphysics, however, has opened a pioneering field that is ready to be tapped to solve all problems. The reason we don't see the answers is because our range of understanding is limited to the parameters of science. Yet if we accept only those parameters, we ignore the spiritual dimension completely.

Concentrating only on physical cures such as quitting drinking does not really lead to recovery—it is an attempt to control the disease. The damage may be superficially repaired, but the underlying causes are not cured. We can't *conquer* alcoholism—we must uncover the true source of the problem. Alcoholic recovery programs that focus on symptoms rather than causes fall short. We have to know the cause to treat the addiction successfully. And ironically, if treated successfully, alcoholism can make us better people than we would have been if we had never had the disease.

Alcoholism is a spiritual disease; it symbolizes a conflict between the soul and the personality. Our negative human-made addictions always exist in relationship to their spiritual counterparts; they complete and explain each other. Each by itself cannot be readily understood. Until we know the positive quality the addiction is attempting to mask, we cannot come to an understanding of the addiction. If we are too hung up on the addiction, we can see no positive quality attached to it. This is the problem. Each of us must attempt to understand the one truth behind the duality by asking ourselves, "Who am I? What am I seeking? What part of me was emerging or retreating that made me sink into alcoholism?" Alcoholism is a miscreation of the soul's intent. It is caused by a spiritual predicament, and its meaning cannot be contained in definitions.

Alice Bailey, author of twenty-four books on the ancient wisdom of metaphysics, lists the causes of the disease as (1) emotional problems, (2) etheric-body transmissions (problems caused by energy shifts in the etheric body), (3) wrong thoughts, (4) overall psychological problems, and (5) karma.[3] The two I will focus on here are numbers 1 and 5.

One strongly supported theory suggests that addiction is caused by the failure to satisfy emotional needs. This is true, but it is only a partial truth. There are more components to alcoholism than just emotional frustration. For example, an expansion of consciousness leads to a growth and expansion of awareness. Expansions of consciousness can be scary for us because they mean we are facing the unknown, so we may retreat into an addiction.

The Law of Karmic Balancing

According to Bailey, the whole subject of disease could be treated from the point of view of karma. She says our psychic and psychological tendencies are inherited from previous lives and are responsible for our current situations.

The law of karma, according to Hindu philosophy, states that everything in the universe must be balanced out: if I do something good, it will come back to me; if I harm someone,

I will be harmed in return. This law also could be translated as "An eye for an eye" or "As you shall sow, so shall you reap." Such a cause-and-effect response could be looked upon as punishment, but it really isn't.

The soul seeks through these experiences to evolve to a higher nature. In many lives we set up cause-and-effect relationships, and lessons are either learned or not learned and karma is gradually balanced out. According to one interpretation, if someone dies addicted to something (cigarettes, alcohol, and so on), that person's soul will reincarnate in a later life to complete the addiction and learn the lesson.

Karmic balancing can often explain why we have negative experiences that we feel we don't deserve. If we were to view this from a wider perspective, we would observe the balancing that is taking place. Sometimes this wider perspective is difficult to achieve during earthly life, but we can grasp it more easily through past-life regression therapy, which reveals the soul's lessons.

Actually, karma has nothing to do with morality. It is a fact of nature as expressed in the law of physics stating, "For every action, there is an equal and opposite reaction." In a life previous to this one, we may have had an enormous amount of guilt and self-hatred, so this time we chose a physical body that would allow us to work out these emotions. If such is the case, it can be worthwhile to go back to those lifetimes to see where we were then—to discover our perspectives and understand what prompted us to make the choices we made—and then forgive ourselves.

Disease breaks up areas where our thoughts are crystallized, or fixed, urgently compelling us to heal ourselves. Being a fatal disease, alcoholism brings about problems that press us to seek treatment and work out our emotional problems. This in turn releases our karmic obligations.

Other addictions may not be based upon quite the same urgency. A workaholic may alienate his or her spouse, but often there is little impetus to change as long as the addiction does not have life-threatening consequences. A woman who is overweight may or may not amend her behavior. She will first look to see what consequences it has in her life and then make an adjustment. Smoking is still widely condoned, and until it causes serious health problems, the smoker may not feel motivated to change. Many addictions are interwoven into the fabric of life and are simply tolerated. On the other hand, with alcohol, things get so bad after a while that we know we cannot go on one day longer like this—thus we quit.

As alcoholics, we have chosen an addiction with great stigma. Most of us feel we are guilty, that we deserve to suffer, and that we deserve people's contempt. This is guilt of the most profound kind—guilt that has carried over for many lifetimes and has crystallized. But alcoholism acts as a catalyst, stirring up the mud in the self (the part of us we'd rather not look at), giving us the desire to deal with those issues we have been avoiding for so long. Eventually it can help us push them into the background, cleaning out the inner house to make room for the real self.

Alcoholism is the "dweller on the threshold"—the sum total of our negative tendencies as expressed through the personality. Conquer this and we conquer a great deal. If we weren't alcoholics, would we ever take the opportunity to know ourselves? How many of us would learn how to deal with our emotions and how to relate better to other people? If we weren't alcoholics, we might remain crystallized, making the same mistakes over and over, repeatedly traveling the wheel of karma and traversing countless lives to reach our ultimate goals.

My natal horoscope shows that I have a strong resistance to change. That is partly why, in the past, I preferred to stay stuck where I was. However, my general life pattern has been one of many changes. Especially after I recovered from alcoholism, I had to make a lot of changes to stay sober. I had to grow emotionally and spiritually. Actually, I went through a spiritual, emotional, and psychological death. Alcoholism was the catalyst that got me to move.

The work of Robert G. Bell supports my assertion that alcoholics must become healthier if they want to stay sober.[4] He contends that recovering alcoholics must not only get well, but must become better adjusted than nonalcoholics because they have to learn how to cope with life without the use of alcohol, a tranquilizer that is readily available to others.

Alice Bailey states in *Esoteric Healing* that thought alone does not cause disease.[5] Of course, thought is involved in the process, but it is not the sole or most important agent. Bailey says that disease has always existed, even among the most primitive forms of life and before any human life appeared on Earth.

There is much confusion in the minds of many healers and New Agers today. Changing our thoughts will not in itself cure us of alcoholism. Overcoming disease is a matter of *consciousness;* positive thinking alone will not suffice. Consciousness means the total collection of our thoughts, feelings, and beliefs molded into a structure of awareness, understanding, and knowledge of both the visible and invisible worlds.

The healing power of thought depends to a great extent on consciousness. In general, the more evolved our soul is, the easier it is to cure ourselves. To have perfect health, we must have the consciousness for it. To rely on metaphysics alone is too risky, as John Price wrote in *The Planetary Commission:*

> Regarding the physical body, I believe that we must always work from the standpoint of where we are in consciousness—and not to gamble by taking action that is beyond our belief system. What I am saying is this: God

works both through the metaphysician and the physician; however, healing cannot be complete until the negative patterns in consciousness are corrected.[6]

For example, a subliminal or hypnosis tape with no AA support group will not be effective in itself against a chemical dependency problem. The main causes of the disease must be dealt with.

Why is it that some healings don't work? It could be that on some level we don't truly desire the healing—we still feel we should suffer, perhaps—or that there is a karmic lesson to be learned from the illness. Each one of us is surrounded by an aura (an electromagnetic shield of energy), and if we desire the healing, the shield will permit the cleansing light to enter and raise our vibrations. However, it is possible to shield ourselves from these positive influences if we cannot let go of the illness or if we have doubts about the healing process itself. To change health permanently, we must change our consciousness by becoming more identified with the God within.

If you are an alcoholic and want to know the cause of your alcoholism, ask yourself, "What am I getting out of drinking?" It might be that you have a desire to control others, or a fear of having to take charge of your life, or an unwillingness to accept responsibility for your actions. Very often as drinkers we are not aware of our real motives; often we do not wish to truly see or heal ourselves. If that is the decision, it must be accepted; this is part of understanding the role that acceptance plays in the process. If an alcoholic makes a decision to die of alcoholism, that is his or her karmic choice. Perhaps that person does not yet realize that we all have an inborn ability to heal ourselves.

In her book *When Society Becomes an Addict*, psychotherapist Anne Wilson Schaef argues that the moral deterioration we see in our society is caused by addictions—whether to alcohol, nicotine, drugs, sex, or food. She says that society as a whole has become an addictive system, and that this system (a horrendous thoughtform) has all the characteristics and processes of an individual alcoholic, including reliance on the defense mechanisms of denial, habitual lying, and the need to control everyone and everything. She defines an addiction as anything leading to obsessive-compulsive behavior, self-deception, and lying to others. We don't want to deal with our feelings, so we choose an addiction to deaden those feelings. We become addicted so we don't have to take responsibility for ourselves—we delude ourselves into thinking someone or something will come along to make things better. We give our power to a substance outside ourselves. Rather than looking for a way to change, we become more conservative, more complacent, and more defensive of the status quo.

Schaef also maintains that addictive relationships (defined in chapter 11) are the norm for our culture, and that our culture has encouraged and fostered these types of relationships. New research in the field of chemical dependency has uncovered how those sharing their lives with addictive people, almost without exception, become addictive people themselves. This is not to say that they become addicted to the same chemical, although this is frequently the case. What is becoming more apparent and predictable is that they are likely to become hooked to addictive patterns of behavior.

Formerly this type of addictive behavior was thought to be the result or natural consequence of living in abusive environments and was given the name "co-dependence." Now we are discovering that it is a disease in itself. In her book *Co-dependence: Misunderstood, Mistreated,* Schaef states, "What we are calling co-dependence is, indeed, a disease that has many forms and suppressions that grow out of a disease process that are inherent in the system in which we live. I call this disease process the addictive process."[7]

There is a tendency to think that what is viewed as "normal" in our society must be that way because everyone is doing it. In the Middle Ages it was considered "normal" to tie up a woman by her thumb and toe and throw her into a lake. If she floated, she was considered a witch, and if she drowned she was considered innocent. "Normal" is something that varies from culture to culture and from historical period to historical period. Co-dependent behavior is widely accepted in our culture, which can make it even more difficult to treat than alcoholism.

Schaef also posits that the addictive system will lead to total destruction, as it has a nonliving orientation. In order to belong to this system, we have to give up our true sense of identity, our power, and our awareness. As I will explain further later, lack of identity is also one of the causes of alcoholism. Accepting the ideas of parents, schools, churches, and society causes us to accept a false image of ourselves. This is known as the "false self." (There will be more information on this in chapter 5.) The fact that most of us have a false sense of identity also contributes immensely to our addiction problems as a society.

There is a little bit of the alcoholic in all of us. Recovery involves putting sobriety first—before our jobs, our mates, and even our children—for sobriety is another word for sane living.

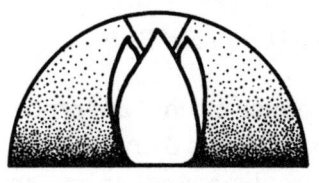

TWO

Comparison of Recovery Programs

The National Council on Alcoholism estimates that there are 18.3 million adult "heavy" drinkers in the United States, around 12.1 million of whom have one or more symptoms of alcoholism. There are many programs that try to deal with these afflicted people, but before comparing these programs I would like to discuss the disease a bit further.

More than 140 research studies indicate a higher incidence of alcoholism in families where one or more members have been diagnosed as alcoholic. In general these studies indicate that a child of an alcoholic father or mother has two to four times the probability of becoming an alcoholic than a child of a nonalcoholic.

The genetic basis of alcoholism has been traced to the deficiency of aldehyde dehydrogenase, an enzyme necessary for the body's disposal of alcohol. Enzymes are the proteins in the body that are responsible for the breakdown and metabolism of food and drugs. They bring about a change, usually a speeding up of bodily processes. Any aberration or alteration in these enzymes is reflected in the way the body disposes of a drug. Supporting this theory are a number of studies that show that certain individuals are genetically predisposed to alcoholism because they metabolize alcohol differently than others.

Women who abuse alcohol are reported to have higher levels of emotional distress than men.They tend to perceive themselves as more depressed, angry, anxious, and lonely. Seventy-four percent of all women alcoholics have experienced sexual abuse.

A study of abstinent alcoholics conducted by Gerard, Saenger, and Wile indicated that the majority of recovering alcoholics are neither happy nor functioning effectively in life.[8] Of those still sober, 54 percent showed signs of emotional disturbance; 24 percent were not functioning effectively in life; and 12 percent were "AA successes" but had acquired little or no social life or identity apart from AA. The remaining 10 percent had achieved a state of integration and personal growth and had "self-actualizing" personalities. Resentment and aggression were observed in all groups with the exception of the self-actualizing one.

In other words, to be successful, an alcoholic must be self-actualizing. Self-actualization is a term coined by psychologist Abraham Maslow referring to the full development of one's abilities and potentials. Following is a chart of Maslow's self-actualizing qualities compared to those qualities that I feel indicate the cessation of personal growth. (Please consult the glossary at the end of the book for any unfamiliar terms.)

Self-Actualizing	*Stagnant*
1. Superior perception of reality	1. Perceiving illusions as facts of life
2. Increased acceptance of self, of others, and of nature	2. Self-hate, condemnation of others
3. Increased spontaneity	3. Lack of spontaneity
4. Increased detachment and desire for privacy	4. Fear of solitude

5. Increased autonomy and resistance to enculturation

5. Dependence on others and inability to think for oneself

6. Freshness of appreciation and richness of emotional reaction

6. Reacting instead of creating responses

7. Higher frequency of peak experiences (mystic experiences)

7. Lack of a spiritual life

8. Increased identification with the human species

8. Feelings of being different or inferior

9. Changed (the clinician would say "improved") interpersonal relationships

9. Participating in destructive relationships

10. More democratic character structure

10. Needing to control everyone and everything

11. Increased creativity

11. Stereotypical thinking

12. Certain changes in the value system

12. Staying stuck in the same rigid value system

13. Increase in problem centering (focusing on solving problems)[9]

13. Self-centered, ego-centric, and gratification oriented

Why the low rate of success with many alcoholic treatment programs? First, some alcoholics perceive sobriety as the most they can achieve. Though often the failure is not personal, it is perceived by the alcoholic as such; even doing all that we can is still not enough to lift entirely the horrendous thoughtform of guilt that hovers over us. But over and over in AA I hear people bemoaning the fact that there must be something wrong with them or they wouldn't be alcoholics: that somehow their alcoholism is *their* fault—a weakness of will, a character defect, or a mental illness. Emotionally these people are stuck at "I am bad; I am guilty; I don't deserve love or kindness." Intellectually they may assent to the disease concept, but not unconsciously. Also, there is the stigma attached to the disease. All this reinforces the guilt thoughtform. A really good book that describes the disease process and this guilt syndrome is *The Hidden Addiction and How to Get Free,* by Janice K. Phelps, M.D., and Alan E. Nourse, M.D.

Remember, just because you are alcoholic, you are not any less a person than someone who is not. In some ways alcoholics are scapegoats for the rest of society. Society often projects its own shadow onto us—that part of itself that it doesn't want to own up to. Keep this in mind next time you contemplate the alcoholism thoughtform. And use this book to help you remove it.

Now, on to a discussion of the programs.

Acupuncture

Though it is estimated that only 15 to 20 percent of chemically dependent addicts ever receive treatment at all, there are many treatment programs available for alcoholics. One is acupuncture, and a number of studies have shown it to be effective in preventing a relapse in alcohol addiction.

In May 1987 a study was conducted by Dr. Milton Bullock at the Hennepin County Detox Center in Minneapolis.[10] Bullock's investigation centered on a randomized study of acupuncture performed on a group of fifty-four hard-core alcoholic recidivists (people who relapse). The results were very encouraging. The patients in the treatment group felt less need for alcohol and had fewer drinking relapses and admissions to the detox center. The majority of the participants who received acupuncture felt that it had a definite impact in lessening their desire to drink.

Acupuncture balances the kundalini energy (discussed in chapter 7), which is a prime concept in understanding alcoholism. If you are depending on your own power to kick the addiction, acupuncture helps a great deal, and I strongly recommend it.

Holistic Systems

There are also holistic substance-abuse treatment centers. For example, the 3HO Superhealth System and Anthropological Techniques consider the whole person, providing therapies to heal the body, mind, and spirit of the recovering addict.

The 3HO Superhealth program in Tucson, Arizona, inspired by the teachings of Yogi Bhajan, has been offering alternative medical-care services for substance abuse since 1973. In 1978, 3HO received the distinction of being the only holistic substance-abuse facility to be accredited as a hospital by the Joint Commission on Accreditation of Hospitals. In addition, Superhealth is a Blue Cross/Blue Shield provider and is accepted by most major insurance companies.

The Superhealth facility is licensed to accommodate eighteen people and now occupies a large commercial-residential facility on the University of Arizona campus, with an additional outpatient clinic capacity of thirty to fifty people. The Superhealth program consists of a highly structured daily format with up to four hours of yoga and meditation supplemented by massage, reflexology, counseling, hydrotherapy, nutritional assessments, communication skills, and vegetarian diets. The intention is to address the problems underlying the addiction.

Yoga is used to release the stresses on the physical body caused by emotions. Superhealth claims a success rate for recovery of 91 percent, based on results of a study completed in July 1986 of graduates from the preceding three years. In other words, 91 percent of these graduates claimed they were still drug or alcohol free. This type of treatment is clearly the way of the future.

Women for Sobriety

Another current program is the Women for Sobriety (WFS) or New Life program, which is a recovery program for women alcoholics. It is based on the idea that the psychology of women is different from that of men. Its founder, Dr. Jean Kirkpatrick, a recovering alcoholic, left AA searching for a program emphasizing self-esteem and women's psychological needs. She created a self-actualizing program that emphasizes emotional growth.

Contemplating the ideas of Thoreau and Emerson, Kirkpatrick wrote the program for WFS, which contains twelve statements. Following is a chart comparing the statements of AA and WFS:

Alcoholics Anonymous	*Women for Sobriety*
1. We admitted we were powerless over alcohol—that our lives had become unmanageable;	1. I have a drinking problem that once had me.
2. Came to believe that a Power greater than ourselves could restore us to sanity;	2. Negative emotions destroy only myself.
3. Made a decision to turn our will and our lives to the care of God as we understood him;	3. Happiness is a habit I will develop.
4. Made a searching and fearless moral inventory of ourselves;	4. Problems bother me only to the degree I permit them to.
5. Admitted to God, to ourselves, and to another human being the exact nature of our wrongs;	5. I am what I think.

6. Were entirely ready to have God remove all these defects of character;

6. Life can be ordinary or it can be great.

7. Humbly asked him to remove our shortcomings;

7. Love can change the course of my world.

8. Made a list of all persons we had harmed and became willing to make amends to them all;

8. The fundamental object of my life is emotional and spiritual growth.

9. Made direct amends to such people whenever possible, except when to do so would injure them or others;

9. The past is gone forever.

10. Continued to take personal inventory, and when we were wrong, promptly admitted it;

10. All love given returns twofold.

11. Sought through prayer and meditation to improve our conscious contact with God as we understood him, praying only for knowledge of his will for us and the power to carry that out;

11. Enthusiasm is my daily exercise.

12. Having had a spiritual awakening as the results of these steps, we tried to carry this message to alcoholics, and to practice these principles in all our affairs.[11]

12. I am competent as a woman and have much to give others.[12]

The WFS program does not emphasize spirituality (at least the group in Riverside, California, did not). If you use this program, don't neglect spirituality, as alcoholism is primarily a spiritual disease. (For information write: Women for Sobriety, Inc., P.O. Box 618, Quakertown, PA 18951.)

Alcoholics Anonymous

The most successful recovery program so far is Alcoholics Anonymous, which is the twelve-step program listed on the left in the preceding chart. AA is a planned program following the steps that commence with the surrendering of the little self and identification with the higher self. Most people in AA are still attuned to an external god, but an adjustment could be made for substituting the higher self for an external god.

However, this can be at times both dangerous and confusing. It is hard for a newly recovering alcoholic to contact his or her higher self, as the withdrawal of alcohol from the body cells influences moods and color perceptions for up to two years after a person becomes abstinent. Alcoholism has permitted the lower self to gain control and has increased the separation between the higher self and the emotional body. The "touch" of the higher self can be subtle and is hard to interpret as such—a person often needs guidance in making a connection with it. (Later in this book we will talk more about this.) There are those who say they have never felt a connection with the higher self; however, everyone has had the connection sometime, but not everyone retains an awareness of it.

Many recovering alcoholics in AA only intellectualize the program, completing the third step yet making no effort toward the hard task of purifying themselves (steps four through ten) or even of taking a long, deep look at themselves, which is what is done in steps four and five.

The fourth step, making a searching and fearless moral

inventory of oneself (an essential step in any recovery program), differs according to where each one of us is on the path. Most people in AA have not found their true selves yet. They define themselves by their roles, and by how other people view them, thinking this is the only reality. Farther on the path, however, we discover that our roles are not us and that another person's perception of us is not who we really are. Social psychologists say there are three selves: the self others see, the one we ourselves see, and the one we really are.

When we take step four we must be prepared for the purification that occurs when the higher self cleans house. This can often be painful. With time I have come to know intuitively what the false self is—how I project it and how it is interpreted. The false self consists of what we think of ourselves based on how others see us and the roles we play in society. It is the fourth step that facilitates the removal of the karma of the false self. It may be painful, but it is permanently rewarding.

There is also the danger that in doing the fourth step we may create more guilt. I know a woman in AA who complained that taking the fourth step brought on a drinking relapse. Use caution when taking this step. If an alcoholic does not have sufficient self-esteem or is guilt ridden, taking this step could be dangerous. Alcoholics can tolerate only a very small amount of guilt, and are often so guilt ridden that they are eager to take this step and do so unprepared. It serves the same function as confession in the Catholic church. Then, too, most recovering alcoholics don't have a realistic idea of what their faults are. The fourth step is hard for anyone.

What is needed is a plan for systematically removing faults—it should be done as painlessly as possible, avoiding extremes. With the fourth step it is necessary to differentiate between the faults that are really ours and the ones that people say we have. Culture plays a heavy part in our interpretation of things.

With regard to the fifth step, I agree with taking responsibility for my actions, but I disagree with the idea of "telling all" and dwelling on faults. I get the impression that some people in AA feel that taking responsibility for one's actions means publicly deprecating oneself. This is where balancing pairs of opposites becomes very important. When there is a lack of balance in AA, we often see an extreme position taken in regard to humility. While humility is a good thing, being extreme about this virtue will only give rise to other faults. Humility reinforces guilt. When my self-esteem is low, I become overly humble, disparaging myself. This, in turn, elicits more feelings of guilt.

A study done on people who used the self-actualizing methods of Maslow showed a balanced perspective with regard to the treatment of opposites. Instead of experiencing a pride/humility dichotomy, we can work for self-acceptance.

There is a tendency for all of us to view our drinking years as a complete waste. The fact is, all my experiences, including my years of drunkenness, have been perfect. They have provided me with the foundation for an understanding of human suffering. I now have oodles of compassion and am prepared for a life of service.

While I was drinking, I was handling my problems the best way I knew how. The esoteric point of view is that there is always growth in any condition in life. In my case, it may have been slow; nevertheless, it was growth. Some alcoholic counselors maintain that there can be no growth at all while one is still drinking. They, too, are polarized in a good/bad, either/or kind of thinking. The new-paradigm approach is to see growth in all conditions. However, the disease must be accepted unconditionally in order to progress. Otherwise we will remain polarized in an "I am bad, I am guilty, I am no good" kind of thinking.

Lucille Cedercrans has some worthwhile reflections on the growth of consciousness in her collected teachings, *The Nature of the Soul:*

> Consciousness grows through its ability to adapt to the changing conditions about it. Contrary to average thought, it is not resistance which produces growth, but rather adaptation, that capacity which allows consciousness to lend itself to a manifesting condition and to come through whole and unharmed. This can be seen in war, in the case of bodily harm such as the removal of a limb, and even in the case of insanity. The consciousness grows because of the experience, not in spite of it. Even though a man be unconscious of this innate ability to adapt, he constantly does so, and when the adaptation can be conscious, we see rapid growth.[13]

Later, Cedercrans goes on to say:

> In other words, if his condition is one of ill health, of poverty, etc., he stops resisting and consciously adapts, asking, "What is the lesson to be learned here? Why has my soul projected me into this situation?" He withdraws the persona from the field of action for a time and reenters as the observer. He quietly enters into his environment, seeing in it only the good, the true and the beautiful, seeking out the growth provided by the condition. And slowly but surely the environment responds to the flood of positive energy exerted upon it. With the new change, the consciousness again adapts.[14]

The truth is, then, we are creating our future right now by the choices we make, and we have a wise self within us that will guide us to the next right step, if we will but be still and listen.

AA steps six to eleven have to do with forgiveness and making amends. Forgiving ourselves and others is essential for progress on the path (more on this in chapter 11). The twelfth step leads to a life of service or a service activity based on helping other alcoholics.

If you think that you are alcoholic, consider this: If you feel AA is not for you, examine your motives. Is it the program itself or simply denial that you have the disease? Perhaps no recovery program would do for now. On the other hand, if you get a strong urge to drink and there is no one to talk to, remember: AA is there whenever you want it.

Other Groups

If you still feel that AA is not for you, you might want to consider alternatives such as private counseling, aversion therapy, or acupuncture treatments. A support group is necessary even if you use the principles of this book.

One group is Al-Anon; its only requirement is that you have a spouse, relative, or friend who is alcoholic. The twelve-step program is utilized but is not as structured. Interpretations are often quite flexible, and groups are smaller and more informal than AA.

There are also new co-dependent groups forming around the country that follow a twelve-step program. The groups in Riverside, California, use Melody Beattie's book *Co-Dependent No More.* The term "co-dependent" is loosely defined in this organization. It could refer to one who is married to an overeater, an alcoholic, a workaholic, or even a sex addict, and so on. In other words, it's not just for relatives of alcoholics.

Adult Children of Alcoholics also follows the AA program. This group's focus is on how to nourish the inner child.

The best kind of group for you depends on your individual preference. There are five types of group therapy:

1. Self-help groups, like those that follow the twelve-step programs;
2. Topic-oriented discussion groups (such as Women for Sobriety);

3. Support groups, which are similar to discussion groups but tend to focus more on current events in the lives of the group members than on a course of topics;
4. Experiential group therapy, which uses techniques such as guided imagery, psychodrama, Gestalt, body-movement exercises, and so on, to unblock feelings (techniques that are particularly valuable when more verbally oriented therapies are unable to reach a person's emotions);
5. Interactional groups, which focus on the spontaneous events that occur during the meetings themselves. (Usually the focus in these groups is on the relationships among the group members.)

In selecting a group, keep these guidelines in mind:

1. The group must be nonjudgmental and nonshaming. If the group does not feel right to you, leave.
2. The group should be democratic and noncontrolling. Each person should be able to be who he or she is.
3. The leader of the group should be reasonably healthy, and he or she must be accepting of the group members.
4. The group should allow for the full expression of all emotions. Without this important dynamic, no one can progress.

I would strongly suggest that you participate in some group—trying to do it alone doesn't work.

Nongroup Options

Another alternative is individual therapy. With individual therapy the focus is totally on you and the relationship between you and your therapist. This approach is recommended for those who have trouble opening up in a group. A therapist has skill in releasing blocked-up emotions. Individual therapy offers the opportunity to allow someone else to parent you, if only symbolically, and to finish the unfinished business between you and your parents.

Another option is past-life regression and therapy. Past-life therapy offers the opportunity to remove unproductive habit patterns by recalling the past-life experience directly related to these patterns. Past-life regression creates a situation where the entire gestalt can be viewed and revised according to your present-day needs.

In *Eye of the Centaur* and *Heart of the Christos,* Barbara Hand Clow uses past-life regression as a tool for spiritual transformation. She recalls her past lives and attunes to experiences of initiation into higher energies. By reliving these experiences, she is able to integrate these higher energies back into her present consciousness.

When we go into a past life, we understand the consciousness we had at that time, and we understand our point of view—that it had to be OK for us to do what we did; otherwise we wouldn't have done it. This knowledge releases judgment, guilt, and fear.

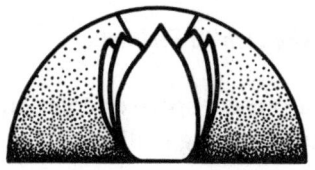

THREE

Functions of Alcoholism

There is some confusion between the cause of something and the function of it; sometimes what we think is the cause is really the function. Knowledge of the *function* of alcoholism—that is, the role it plays in our lives—is essential in transforming the disease.

Addiction is not evil; it is a mere narrowing of perspective, a false way of looking at ourselves and our world. We believe we are somebody we are not. The following definitions are clues to the functions of alcoholism. In them are also clues to finding our true identities.

1. Addiction is nongrowth. It is being stuck in the past—going through the same patterns over and over. Addiction sets in when a normal urge has been frustrated. It can be perceived as blocked creative energy.
2. Addiction is postponement. It is repetitive. What we did yesterday, we are doing today through force of habit. We postpone giving up the addiction, we postpone doing something better with our lives, and tomorrow often never comes.
3. Addiction is an attachment to something outside ourselves. We give up our power to a substance so that it will give us what we think we need.
4. Addiction is a technique to get out of the present-

time and/or present-space orientation. It is a
technique for avoiding reality.

Getting into a present-time and/or present-space orientation is extremely important. As alcoholics, we are usually centered in the future or the past. Projecting into the future can cause anxiety, because we don't know what tomorrow holds. Therefore, it is best to stay in the present time and just deal with that. Being focused in the past can arouse regrets and guilt, and it detracts from our ability to deal with the present. Living in a present-time and/or present-space orientation will reduce conflicts and center us, making us less prone to relapses.

Our current cultural attitudes play a large part in the way we perceive alcoholism, the way it affects us, and our responses to treatment. Perceiving the disease in an almost entirely negative way has much to do with the way we respond to recovery. We have the responsibility of finding the supreme positive in even the most negative situation.

Perhaps you've heard the statement that our greatest strengths are born out of the substance of our greatest weaknesses. Experiences with our greatest weaknesses can bring out the worst in us and at the same time elicit opportunities for a growth yet unrealized. We may feel that alcoholism is a blight on our souls, but we must remember that the blackest shadow in us is cast by a corresponding light of the same degree. We must get the shadow and the light to work together to transform the addiction.

To transform the disease we need to know what aspect of ourselves was trying to emerge when life became so intolerable that we chose the bottle instead. Were we afraid to think, to feel, to be? Our addiction is our teacher—it will show us what was trying to emerge. Perhaps we thought we needed a mate to define us, so we drank to cure loneliness. However, we do not need another person to define us when we are truly ourselves.

What was your own addiction masking? Some possibilities include creativity, compassion, a life of service to humanity, self-autonomy, self-actualization, intellectual development, and the courage to live your life in the present moment with no crutches.

With me it was creativity, a side of me that had been suppressed due to my childhood trauma. My creativity didn't manifest until I was in my forties. Before that I had no real identity, no sense of who I was. I could always think independently, but creativity eluded me until I finally used it to get in touch with myself and my feelings.

Addiction is misdirected creative energy. Studies show that there is a correlation between alcoholism and creativity. Too often addicts in recovery feel a sense of stagnation and malaise, with no clear awareness of who they are in the moment. Creativity helps enormously to recover this missing sense of self.

Another side of me that was emerging when alcoholism took over was my intellectual side. I had begun to question authority and traditional mores and norms. I was forming a new center within myself to evaluate experience. But I was afraid of my intellect, afraid of thinking. Alcoholism drew me deeper into the convictions and ideas of the mass mind. Like most alcoholics, I was less able to shield myself from those ideas while I was drinking, and they began to affect me. It was easier to go along with the crowd. Thinking made me feel uncomfortable; I was afraid to be myself because I might be considered "different." It took courage to be myself. I knew that if I learned who I was, I would have to live up to my convictions and be responsible for them, and that scared me.

Once we know what qualities the addiction is masking, we can take steps to let go of it. When we decide to let go of the addiction by the act of surrender to the higher self, we attract to us from within the qualities of the true self. These qualities will then be drawn out and we will manifest them naturally. To transform any addiction, it is essential to do this. This is the crucial element that is lacking in conventional treatment programs—and the one that for me, at least, made all the difference.

FOUR

How Addiction Unfolds in the Personality

An understanding of how the lower self and partial selves operate is essential to understanding addiction. The lower self controls addiction. We must learn to discriminate between the higher self and the partial selves that are only portions of our personality.

The lower self is only a part of us, but often we are so caught up in the mundane world that it is all we are conscious of. It is the lower self that is addicted, and we must be able to recognize how it operates. The following list can help to identify its characteristics:

1. The lower self is interested only in getting its physical needs met in one way or another. This is good; our needs have to be fulfilled or we can become addicted.
2. The lower self is not controlled by the higher self; it is controlled by the ego, with the exception of some extremely evolved people.
3. The reactions of the lower self are based on past programming from the subconscious mind.
4. The lower self is a reaction to life's experiences. It does not consciously create anew.
5. The behaviors of the lower self are all learned.

6. The lower self is emotionally attached to life, seeking status and power.
7. The lower self is not able to stand aside from its experiences and evaluate them. It says, "My experiences are who I am." These experiences then totally determine our actions.
8. The lower self is dominated by feelings of lack, limitation, and scarcity.
9. The lower self emphasizes our isolated, separate state.
10. However, the lower self is also our access to present time. It keeps us anchored in the present moment and in physical reality. Alcoholism is a tool to avoid our present-time/space domain.

Too often we mistake the lower self for what we really are, unaware that there is a unified self that directs us even though we often do not experience it. Without the aid of the higher self, the lower self becomes too identified with superficial and mundane preoccupations, and we get stuck with our feet in the mud. Our ego-dominated perceptions distort reality, and we create addictions to help us cope.

Of course, the lower self is not all bad. It reminds us when our needs are not being met, keeps the house clean, pays the bills, watches our health, and puts gas in the car. It is a part of who we are. It will get our physical needs satisfied at whatever cost. But it should be guided by the higher self—and with self-actualization, the higher self will indeed assume more and more control.

Here is an example of how I act when I'm letting my lower self rule: I wake up in the morning and it's raining, so I feel bad. I get up and the toast burns, so I feel bad. My daughter comes in, kisses me, talks to me about how well the school play went last night, so I feel good. The mail arrives, and in it is a notice from the utility company that they will be turning off my electricity in two days if I don't pay on time, so I feel bad. A friend calls up and invites me to her house for the weekend, and I feel good again—and on it goes. My moods depend on whatever is going on in the outside world. I am going through life reacting to whatever the external world drops in my lap. This is my lower self.

My lower self can rule me if I let it. But I have another self residing inside me, one that can think for itself and that can choose to react or not. To transform addiction, the lower self and higher self must work together.

When I had my first mystical experience, I threw out my lower self. I became so enraptured with my mystical vision that it was hard to go back to the mundane world, and when I did I tended not to notice what was going on in my environment. At times I was disorganized and less efficient. I disconnected from people, wanting to be alone most of the time.

On the path, we are striving to transcend the ego by meeting its needs on a personal and interpersonal level. Denying these needs will only harm us. We must think enough of ourselves to get these needs met. A soul-dominated person can evolve only with the development of a strong ego and an integrated personality. Again, the higher self and the lower self must work together to make us whole. In most people the personality predominates, but with evolution, the essence or soul will assume control over the personality.

The Integration of the Partial Selves

The course of our life is determined . . . by an array of selves that live within each of us. These selves call out to us constantly—in our dreams and fantasies, in our moods and maladies, and in a multitude of unpredictable reactions to the world around us.[15]
—Hal Stone and Sidra Winkelman

As a recovering alcoholic, I had to work hard at self-acceptance. Part of that work involved the integration of my partial selves. Partial selves are fragments of the personality. Their main purpose is to get our ego needs met; they are not the true self. However, it is not in our best interest to try to rid ourselves of a partial self—even a negative one. One of these partial selves may take over our personality, and our responses will be very mechanical. These partial selves are a part of us; if we attempt to get rid of them, they will become even more problematic. Following is my way of integrating these little selves.

Acknowledgment or recognition: The first step is an awareness of which partial self is operating. You will usually notice a personality change. (For example, "I always react this way to a female in charge.") Picture the little self as it is. Give it a name. See how it looks; see yourself talking to it. Watch its body language, its reactions, and how it expresses itself. Feel its energy.

Once this partial self is identified, start a dialogue with it to find out what it wants and what it is trying to do for you. Talk to the little self as if it were a real person. You will become aware in a short amount of time what this little self is trying to accomplish for you.

Basically, any partial self is simply trying to help you manage a situation that it does not trust you to handle yourself. Ask it what it thinks. Ask it how it wants to change your life. Listen to what it has to say. See the world through its perspective. Feel any new energy it brings to you. Perhaps it can offer solutions to old problems. Then determine if its solution is better than the one you had.

If you feel that your solution is still the better one, convince the little self that you can manage the situation just fine by yourself. Strike up a bargain with it if necessary.

Acceptance: For acceptance to occur, there must be no judgment about these little selves and the parts they play. For example, do not say, "No one likes aggressive females. I'm too controlling." See the partial selves without judgment. All of our parts are OK, and they must be accepted for what they are.

Once you see how these partial selves have been attempting to help you (although in a peculiar manner), you will begin to accept them. You will know that they are parts of your personality structure that need to be integrated. This will also help keep the little selves within their own boundaries. The integration of all parts of the self is primarily a process of self-acceptance. Wholeness results from total self-acceptance. Wholeness is the mark of mental health.

You may be surprised at the new energy you receive from this exercise of acceptance. That is because you are bringing parts of yourself out of hiding.

Cooperation/Coordination: Once you have achieved acceptance, the next step is easy. Judgment will fade away, and you will comprehend the role of these little selves in your personality.

Synthesis: This occurs whenever your need for a little self fades and you feel you can handle a situation by yourself. The little self has then been integrated into your personality and you no longer sense its presence. Emotional overreaction is a hint that you are reacting to a partial self.

Liberating the Lost Inner Child

Nurturing the inner child is extremely important for recovery. It is the child within that we have neglected, and this child will lead us to balance. Physical sobriety is the first part of recovery. With it, we start feeling our emotions again and recovering our self-esteem, but much work still has to be done. If this work is not done, the addiction to alcohol will be transferred to another addiction—food, cigarettes, work, and so forth—and we will still be just as compulsive as before. (I was sober and getting my self-esteem back from group support, but I was still addicted to sugar and developing a weight problem.) The journey to wholeness requires that we make contact with the lost, wounded, inner child that resides in each one of us. That child has been ignored and neglected for a long time. Because of this, the child is egocentric, weak, and frightened.

In order to reconnect with the wounded and hurt child, we have to go back and reexperience the emotions that we have blocked. Our addictions are the result of these old blocked feelings (our unresolved grief) being acted out over and over again. We can either work out these feelings by reexperiencing them, or they will be acted out in an addiction. We can also act them out in extreme ways, such as depression or suicide, or we can project them onto others in the form of blame.

It is not the traumas we suffered in childhood that make us unstable, but our inability to express them. These traumas must first be acknowledged, then expressed, so that they can be released. It is these traumas that make us think little of ourselves. For example, the adult in me may know that I am not to blame, but my child feels she was responsible for the harm that was done to her.

It is the child in us that feels we are guilty and deserving of punishment. Talk to your child as if it were your own little boy or girl. Explain that it is not to blame for what happened. Become a parent to it all over again. Be the good parent your inner child never had.

We recycle our developmental needs all through our lives. If a need was not met, it will reappear again and again until we find a way to fulfill it. If I was neglected in mothering, I can look to my support group for mothering or

nurturing. Or I can become a mother to my wounded child—
the mother she never had.

There are different ways to heal the inner child. To get our
needs met, we can be good to ourselves—treat ourselves
with nurturing, respect, and kindness. In time the child
within will feel loved and appreciated, and will release its
tremendous spiritual power.

FIVE

Identity

At the basis of every addiction is a profound identity crisis: we don't know who we are or how to find ourselves.

Social Identity

In our society, identity is formed from many sources, including job, sex role, parentage, and marriage. For example, there are several sexual identities available to women: marriage and motherhood, being single, or being in a nontraditional partnership. Though definitions of personal identity are a matter of choice, the traditional role of wife and mother is still the most popular.

Most women identify themselves mainly by their primary relationships and secondarily by their work. In general, women perceive themselves in terms of how they relate to other people. A woman's self exists in a social context; it grows and develops as part of an ongoing process of interaction with the social world. To do this, a woman must repress many parts of herself.

Men, too, have repressed parts of themselves. They are taught to develop their intellectual sides and to suppress their emotional-intuitive natures. A man defines himself primarily by his work and his profession. His success or failure is gauged by what he does on the job. Then he may marry, and some part of him becomes husband and father as well. The following paragraph is typical of how an unemployed man might describe himself:

> It's hard. Let's see. I'm a forty-five-year-old man. Most of my life I've been in heavy construction—an operating engineer. You see, right now I can't really describe myself because I'm in a very big transition period. I'm unemployed. The bottom fell out of construction and I haven't worked regularly for two years—only occasionally, and lately not even that. So, you see, I can't say who I am right now.

However, men's roles are changing in society. As women change, men must make adjustments, too, but often their egos don't want to adapt to these changes. Many men have a divided self, have received little or no nurturing, are undeveloped emotionally, and as they grow older often experience spiritual dissatisfaction. Because of these social expectations, it is very difficult for them to form an identity in the mundane world.

Self Identity

We are composed of four bodies: the emotional, physical, mental, and spiritual bodies. Each of these bodies is a separate entity or aspect of ourselves.

The emotional body is the vehicle of consciousness comprised of our feelings and emotions, and it vibrates at a very low frequency. The mental body is the vehicle of consciousness comprised of our thoughts, ideas, mental processes, creativity, and so on. The physical body is our physical form of consciousness existing as part of three-dimensional matter. It is the most dense of the four bodies. The spiritual body is the vehicle of consciousness that is our essence, or soul.

We all have some kind of self-identification. Few people are aware of what this really means and how it affects their lives. There are three levels of self-identification: physical, emotional, and mental. We identify with that which constitutes the greatest value to us or is considered the most important.

Some people place a great deal of emphasis on their physical bodies and the way they look. We are not our physical bodies, yet when a woman has a physical body that she feels is not attractive, she thinks less of herself. This is identification with the physical body.

Instead, self-esteem should rest on our identities as souls. Our true identities are our higher selves. I am not an alcoholic; rather, I am a soul who has a drinking problem. Identification as an alcoholic strengthens the thoughtform as well as all the negativity associated with the disease. A cancer patient does not say, "I am cancer." AA feels that identifying oneself as an alcoholic breaks down the denial system. This is true, but it also has the negative result of rendering alcoholism more powerful. Dwelling on the past also strengthens the alcoholic thoughtform.

Disidentification

Most addicts are so identified with their feeling states that they can't get past them. Identification with the emotional body is widespread and exacerbates addiction problems to no end. We have forgotten who we are and what our destinies are. Disidentification from our emotional states and the work of balancing emotions takes several years. Disidentification is the realization that we are neither our emotions nor our physical bodies. They are part of us but are not the central "I," the essence of each of us. Through meditation, we can perceive this situation more objectively, and creative insights will follow.

Some people are more identified with a role. As I mentioned, many women primarily identify with wifehood and motherhood. When we identify solely with a role, it does not give us a sense of our true selves. Turning to the external world to find ourselves is how we lose ourselves.

A woman I know in AA was going through a painful divorce. She said she was devastated, and that her only identity had been that of wife and mother. When this was gone, she felt there was nothing left. She was encouraged to build up her self-esteem, as her sobriety would be precarious until she could form a more stable identity. Forming a permanent identity with her higher self would give her the self-esteem she so desperately needed. In order to achieve this, she needed to disidentify from her emotional and physical bodies, and indeed from all roles.

Such false self-identification has a couple of consequences:

1. When we identify with a part of our personalities or with one particular role, it diminishes our capacity to identify with our other selves and to integrate all facets of our personalities. Also, because our self-identification changes drastically with time (we grow older, the children leave, etc.), attachment to a particular role brings much conflict.
2. As a result, we don't really know ourselves.

The identity crisis changes as we evolve. We drank because of a false identification with our physical bodies and with our emotional natures. This false identification with our physical and emotional bodies is a primary impediment to lasting sobriety. We don't know who we are and what we are capable of becoming. As Roberto Assagioli says:

> The basis of all self-realization and inner freedom is disidentification. We are dominated by what our self becomes identified with, and we can direct and use whatever we disidentify from.[16]

The only way to achieve real self identity is by observing our emotions. Through this process, these emotions gradually lose their hold and intensity.

There are three parts to disidentification:

1. Observation, done through observing oneself (as in the Observer Self Meditation in the Appendix;
2. Disidentification from the small selves and roles, done through meditation and with the following exercises (and also accomplished through the exercise on partial selves in chapter 4);
3. Reidentification with the soul, done through meditation.

Psychosynthesis, one of the first techniques of Roberto Assagioli, M.D., and one that is widely used in the psychotherapeutic field, is an exercise in disidentification and realization of the self. Practicing it can bring miracles of reorientation in our lives. Its affirmations bring about a clearer sense of the reality of the "I," and we soon become more detached from the pulls, drives, moods, and impulses that used to control us. The following exercise is my adaptation of Roberto Assagioli's affirmations:

Exercise in Disidentification and Realization of the Self

Say to yourself:

> I have a body, but I am not my body. My body may be in sickness or health, rested or tired, but it is not the real self, my true essence. I value it as a means of experience and action, but it is only an instrument. It is not who I am. I treat it well, but I am not my body.

After a short period of reflection and affirmation, proceed with the next two states:

> I have emotions, but I am not my emotions. They are diverse, changing, and sometimes contradictory. They may range from love to hatred, joy to sorrow, and yet they are not my essence. I

remain. Though a wave of anger may submerge me, it will pass; therefore, I am not this anger. Since I can observe and often control my emotions, it is clear that they are not myself. They are part of myself but not the central "I."

I have a mind, but I am not my mind. Its contents are constantly changing; I can observe it, and often it refuses to obey me. It is a valuable tool, but it is not my real self. It is a part of myself, residing in me, but it is not the essence of my being. I have a mind, but I am not my mind.

Next comes self-identification. Affirm thoughtfully:

After disidentifying myself, the "I," from my sensations, emotions, and thoughts, I recognize and affirm that I am a center of pure self-consciousness, a center of will, capable of observing and directing my physical body and all my psychological processes. I am essence.

SIX

Psychic Energetics: Clearing the Auric Field

While we are drinking, we are not able to resist the horrendous thoughtforms generated by the mass mind. As a result, we lose our individuality, our creativity, and our ability to think independently. Thus we come to believe in the illusions of separation and nonunity, because they represent the way humanity thinks. We become conservative and complacent, and strive to maintain the status quo at all costs.

We also expose ourselves to the negativity of the astral dimension, and there is danger in this. The astral dimension is a frequency of time and space beyond the physical dimension that exists simultaneously with the physical plane. It is the astral plane on which the emotions of humanity register collectively.

We each possess an astral body, enveloping our physical body, which is comprised of our emotions and our own auric field. The astral body, also known as the energy body or light body, moves out of the physical body into the astral dimension whenever we are sleeping, or during accidents, trauma, or surgery. It is connected to the physical body by a silver cord (also made of astral matter). The astral body is impregnated with astral energy that has a certain "stickiness" to it. This stickiness attracts other astral energies to us.

Every inanimate object—every home, building, piece of

furniture, article of clothing, and so on—carries traces of the energy of the animate beings to which it has been exposed, including the astral energies of those who made the object, those who sold it, and those who previously owned it. Such energies are impregnated into the fabric of everything that exists.

Moreover, the electromagnetic energy field of every human being interacts with the energy fields of other people and things surrounding it. So, if we spend too much time around someone or something that has a strong negative vibration, we may accept this negativity into ourselves and be affected by it. Once this occurs, our own spiritual vibrations may suffer.

It is important to understand the nature of the astral dimension so we can use it intelligently to help us understand how we interact with energy. Otherwise, astral energy of other beings and things will weaken us and suck our own energy. As we clear our emotional bodies and release energy into the astral dimension, we are healing ourselves and altering the astral plane. Clearing out our own "sticky" astral energy will allow higher consciousness to come in to us.

There are some esotericists who deny the existence of such negative energies, implying that the effects people experience are simply the results of negative thinking. However, these energies are real; they do exist. The aura is the electromagnetic force field surrounding all living things. It can be seen psychically by clairvoyants. Once lower energies are drawn into the aura, they lower its vibration and make a person more emotional, less centered, and even more vulnerable to addictions.

While we are drinking, we are defenseless against these negative energies. They permeate our auras and exert a seductive attraction. The higher self, too, is lost while drinking. Thus, our perceptions of ourselves change. We become aware of feelings that may be completely foreign to our true selves. We may become anxious or prone to emotional disturbances as a result of these energies, which have been allowed to grow on us like parasites. In time, we may experience delirium tremens, a very serious state of withdrawal whose symptoms include severe tremors, agitation, fast pulse, and intense disorientation.

Alcohol in excessive amounts interferes with our centering. Being centered gives us a feeling of being collected at our centers rather than scattered—of being aware and in control of our own personal dynamics. Centering is the ability to calm our own nervous systems and to go deep within our consciousnesses until we achieve a sense of equilibrium.

As alcoholics, we need centering techniques to keep ourselves calm and focused (see chapter 8). We wouldn't have a problem with centering if we were in a present-time-and-space orientation. The second we move out of the present, we are prone to the astral. A lack of ego center is part of the appeal of alcohol and drugs; it allows us to relax, be ourselves, and appear less defensive and hostile. But there is danger in being without a center, for it leaves us open to the astral dimension.

Indiscriminate sex, alcohol, and drugs weaken our auric fields, leaving us open to an invasion of alien energies and in some cases bringing about a leak. This leads to a weakening of will power. We forget our goals, and that keeps us entrapped in the astral dimension, resulting in depression and discouragement.

By drinking, we open ourselves not only to astral invasion but also to psychic attack. A psychic attack is an instance in which we become opposed by a force, energy, or intelligence not on our particular wavelength. Whenever we are immersed in the astral dimension, psychic attack becomes possible.

Following is an example of astral invasion: You wake up in the morning feeling fine. Then a person with a strong negative vibration enters your house; this person is very stressed. If your aura is open at this time, you may absorb this negative energy. This constitutes a form of astral invasion.

Another example: You have been drinking and are feeling pretty good. A person comes into your house who has a violent temper. Pretty soon you find yourself getting increasingly angry. In a drunken state you cannot resist the onslaught of the other person's negative energies—they permeate your aura—and you take on his or her emotions and stresses. This, too, constitutes astral invasion.

Most of the emotions that influence us are not really part of us. They come from the astral dimension. Crowd psychology is one example of this; people do things in a crowd that they would never do as individuals.

However, we fortunately have free will about all this. Most alcoholics find it hard to believe in free will, but the more we believe in it, and the more we use the freedom we have, the less we are prone to astral invasion. As we grow emotionally, we see that we have more choices; our reality does not seem so restricted. While we are drinking, we have a kind of tunnel vision that narrows our choices to just one or two.

Most alcoholics are afraid of freedom and the responsibility it entails. We want our worlds to be safe and secure, so we avoid taking responsibility at all costs. We give our power away to a substance or a person. As alcoholics we have to reclaim our power—it is our birthright.

I was visiting a friend, who was an alcoholic in denial, whom I hadn't seen for about a year. As soon as I entered her house, I noticed and felt negative energies—feelings of hostility and anxiety—even though I had been in a peaceful mood prior to that point. At that time I had about two years of sobriety. I also noticed that my friend had changed markedly in a year. She expressed more resentment and hostility, and she was drinking more. I also had the impression that negative entities had gathered in her home. Soon after seeing her, I started to have pessimistic thoughts myself, and old resentments of my own flared up. Were there entities in her home, which I carried out with me? I definitely believe so. Though I was not able to see these entities, I certainly felt them. I cleared myself of them at once, using a method of self-exorcism recommended by Dr. Edith Fiore in her book, *The Unquiet Dead.*

It takes a certain amount of humility to admit that we are "off track" or under the influence of negative energies. We like to feel that we are special—that "it can't happen to me." Signs of "off trackedness" or negative influence of astral energies to be aware of include:

1. A sapping of your vitality, as if someone or something is sapping your energy.
2. Feeling like doing activities that you wouldn't ordinarily do when you are with a certain person or a group of people.
3. Extreme mood swings or changes in your personality. For example, have your friends commented about your tiredness, a change in your attitude, or a change in your personality?
4. A sudden onset of anxiety or depression that appears to come "out of the blue." For example, you wake up in the morning feeling wonderful, but by 10 a.m. you're feeling very depressed and can't think of one good reason why.
5. Becoming anxious or depressed while you are in the company of a certain person, but the anxiety or depression lifts when the person leaves.

Such astral energies perpetuate our separation from our higher selves. They make us more emotional, coloring our perceptions of reality and making contact with our higher selves more difficult.

Just because some people seem to thrive in a negative psychic atmosphere without noticing such energies doesn't mean that nothing is there. For example, at this very moment you are probably in a room through which radio and TV waves are flowing, yet you do not feel them. So it is with some people; they may not feel negative energies, but the energies are certainly there. They have been seen and felt by clairvoyants. In some people the threshold between the conscious and unconscious minds is very dense, so they don't sense such things. However, they may have feelings of irritability and depression that lift when they leave a place.

Notice when somebody makes you feel bad, as happened to me upon visiting the house of my friend. This is a sign of astral invasion. So, too, are your own negative thoughts often a sign of astral invasion. If you have mediumistic abilities, you may also experience poltergeist phenomena, such as disappearing objects, mysterious breakages, and so forth.

There is no point in trying to sensitize yourself to these energies; the alcoholic is emotionally sensitive enough already. The important thing is to form within yourself some kind of protection against these extraneous energies. My hypothesis is that allowing these astral energies to grow on you will make you more prone to greater and more continuous invasion by them, which in turn will suck away your ability to resist drinking. I also believe that ignorance of the laws of psychic defense is often a factor leading to relapse after one has obtained temporary sobriety. The best psychic defense is simply to avoid negative people and circumstances and to surround yourself with positivity. Once the psychic atmosphere is cleared, then you can concentrate on rebuilding your physical health and personality.

According to many individuals experienced with psychic phenomena, spirit obsession or possession is another reason that alcoholics find it hard to stop drinking. Spirit obsession occurs when an earthbound entity from the lower, nonphysical planes psychically transfers feelings, desires, hang-ups, or thoughts to a still-living person.

I believe that when we view negative thoughtforms as manifestations of being possessed, we are better able to deal with them. We do not know exactly what is happening, but if we personalize such energies into unwanted entities, we are better able to eliminate them.

Another way of viewing these entities is to see them as part of our shadow sides. Our shadows contain everything about ourselves that we want to deny—most often, negative traits we don't wish to own up to. They are usually what our families, society, and we ourselves consider bad and shameful. Our shadows could also be our good sides that we are denying. For example, a creative child growing up in a noncreative family may stifle his or her creativity.

We suppress the shadow, but it comes back out when we least expect it. Alcoholism causes its release. An example is the loving husband who, after years of drinking, becomes violent. Many crimes are committed under the influence of alcohol that never would be committed otherwise. We ignore the shadow, yet it screams out for attention.

Then, too, we may drink to keep certain traits hidden. Facing up to our shadows is painful, but it is the only way to become whole. The shadow should be integrated into our psyches. The entities we feel are separate from us may be only our shadows; we may perceive them as separate entities, but they are really parts of ourselves. However, it actually doesn't matter whether such astral thoughtforms are actual entities or parts of our shadow selves; what matters is how we feel about them. While we are addictive, these energies will continue to haunt us until we face up to them and incorporate them into our psyches.

In *The Unquiet Dead*, psychologist Edith Fiore writes that one of the strongest ties binding departed spirits to the physical world is addiction—to alcohol, drugs, sex, even food.[17] According to Fiore, departed spirits with addictions cluster around living addicts so they can partake in their addictions again. She believes in such entities and uses the word "possession" throughout her book. However, this is not really the right word to describe this phenomenon, for individuals have the potential for free will about what is occurring.

Fiore says there are degrees of spirit obsession ranging from nearly total takeover (in which case the original spirit is absent most of the time) to minor influence on the personality. Some of the factors that appear to influence the degree of a person's vulnerability to outside energies are alcohol and drug use, stress, depression, fear, illness, anger, and the intrinsic strength of the person compared to that of the alien entity. Any strong negative emotion lowers the vibration of the aura, making a person temporarily vulnerable. Fatigue, exhaustion, and illness also temporarily weaken the aura's protective capacity.

In a high majority of cases, Fiore writes, afflicted individuals are unaware of their obsessions. She believes that use of the Ouija board or automatic writing actually invites this type of problem. People use these activities hoping that they will attract higher entities, but often they attract the lower ones instead.

Use of the Ouija board is dangerous in the extreme—it is a doorway to the lower astral plane. The entities contacted on this plane belong to the group of souls who have recently died and have not had the benefits of higher-self teachings in the afterlife.

Automatic writing is another practice that invites spirits to attach to the aura. In this system, writing is performed by spirits that control the hands of living persons. This can be done with a pencil, pen, typewriter, or word processor. This practice, too, can attract any kind of spirit.

Fiore says that channeling invites spirits to become attached to the aura as well. A person may lament, "I only wanted good spirits to come through; I didn't expect a negative one." However, when we invite spirits to come, unless we are very careful, almost any kind of spirit can enter us and stay. Anyone who is under the influence of alcohol and drugs should definitely not channel or invite spirits for visits. Drinking and abusing drugs are invocations in their own rights, and no amount of positive affirmations or protection can guarantee positive influences.

In *The Unquiet Dead,* Dr. Fiore lists the ten most common signs of possession, which you might experience as follows:

1. You have a persistently low energy level that doesn't seem to have a physical or emotional cause.
2. You experience extreme mood swings or changes in your personality. Do people remark that you are like "another person"? Do you think, "This is not like me"? Have you suddenly acquired habits that are "out of character"?
3. Inner voices speak to you. It is hard to differentiate which thoughts are yours and which thoughts are from an obsessing entity. Only those who are clairaudient (have the ability to psychically hear voices that are inaudible to most people) can hear spirit voices and distinguish them from their own.
4. If you abuse drugs and alcohol, Dr. Fiore contends, you can be sure there are spirits around you. She said that every one of the patients she treated who abused alcohol or drugs was bothered by these entities.
5. You are impulsive and do things without thinking. All alcoholics are impulsive, but does this extend to activities such as going on extravagant shopping sprees, running up gambling debts, and so on? If so, this may be the spirits indulging themselves.
6. You have "blackouts," or breaks in consciousness.

Do you forget whole hours, even days?
7. You have problems with concentration. Is it hard for you to stay with mental activities? Do you feel like you're in a fog most of the time?
8. You experience sudden anxiety or depression. Sometimes this appears to come from "out of nowhere." You may be picking up the feelings of other spirits that are manifesting through you.
9. You have difficulty recuperating from illness. If recently hospitalized, did you have an unusually difficult time recovering? Did you develop any new pains or symptoms after your hospitalization that appeared to be unrelated to your condition? Serious illness weakens your aura's protective capacity.
10. You experience emotional and/or physical reactions to reading *The Unquiet Dead*.

This is how to score:

> No problem; not noticed: 0
> Sometimes; not a big problem: 1
> Always, most of the time, or yes: 2

Fiore says that a score of 10 or more suggests spirit obsession—especially when combined with a score of 2 on items 2, 3, 4, or 10. If you obtained a score of less than 10, use your judgment; it does not necessarily mean there is no problem.

Until you have awareness of this negative-entity dynamic, you will be weakened by it. It will drain most of your energy, leaving you more vulnerable to a drinking relapse. Negative entities frequent bars because there is an abundance of negative energy there. Sometimes you can get rid of these entities if you ignore them. Other times it may be necessary for you to demand that they leave. If you do go into a bar, consciously leave them there when you depart. Fiore gives a self-exorcism technique in her book that is very helpful. (An exorcism is an attempt to dislodge an alien spirit from one's aura.)

A bar may get a bad name for intoxicated customers and close down. If a new bar opens up in the same location, even with new management and new customers, the "old trouble" may start up again. No one who suspects he or she is an alcoholic should visit such a place. In fact, if you suspect you are alcoholic, it's best not go into any bar.

In her book, *Ecstasy Is a New Frequency*, Chris Griscom proposes a technique to strengthen your aura, clear your emotional body, and protect yourself from the invasion of astral energy. She recommends extending light energy out from the top of your head and through your solar plexus, and letting it flow out all around you. When the light energy radiates out, you're stripping away emotional residues that could have attracted all kinds of negative astral energies.

Protective techniques are necessary in the early stages of recovery. Once we have reclaimed our freedom, cleared out our auric fields, healed our emotional bodies, and merged with our higher selves, we will have raised our vibrations sufficiently so that these energies will no longer be attracted to us.

For those of you who suspect there are entities attached to your auras, I am going to offer some methods of psychic defense. These techniques can also be used to clear a negative atmosphere after a family quarrel or other emotional turmoil. The best sources I can recommend for such techniques are Dion Fortune's *Psychic Self-Defense* and Edith Fiore's *The Unquiet Dead*.

An effective way of clearing a negative psychic atmosphere in a house is to scatter or sprinkle garlic. Leave it overnight, then in the morning gather it up and burn it. Another practice is to place an onion in a vase on the fireplace as if it were a hyacinth bulb. Do this whenever unpleasant visitors are expected. As soon as they have left, burn the onion, which will have absorbed the negative vibrations. You also might consider not allowing unpleasant visitors into your space.

Interviewing people who are intimidating will work better if you imagine yourself separated from them by a sheet of plate glass. You can see and hear them, but their vibrations cannot reach you. If you feel someone may be trying to harm you in some way, imagine yourself separated from them by a brick wall. That person's positive energy will still flow through the wall; the barrier keeps out only negativity.

It is important to set up boundaries between ourselves and other people. In that way we can avoid their negative energies. Alcoholics, it has been said, have boundary problems; we came from dysfunctional homes and never learned to set them. Boundaries are limits that say, "This is how far I will go. This is what I will do or won't do for you. This is what I won't tolerate from you." Once we know our boundaries, we are less prone to astral invasion.

Finally, when a person is intimidating you, realize that it is that person's problem, not yours. You didn't cause it, and that person is responsible for his or her own problem. Don't get emotionally involved with it. There is more on setting boundaries in chapter 11.

It is also important to remember that your aura is open while you are sleeping, while you are in meditation, and when you get very emotional. This is one reason it is important not to drink: you may develop a leaking aura because you are more emotional. If you sense a psychic disturbance, discontinue all psychic practices and go back to the prayers of your childhood or ask your higher self for protection. According to some people experienced in psychic phenomena, the prayers of our childhoods are very effective as a form of psychic protection.

It is a good idea when trying to break an undesirable psychic contact to immerse yourself in a bath that has been specifically consecrated for that purpose. You can buy either prepared baths or make your own. Many people bathe ritually to cleanse themselves of any negative spiritual influence that has become part of their auras. These baths promote healing. They also clear the emotional body, neutralizing negative emotions.

If you want to take a spiritual bath, first take a shower to get rid of the dirt, then clean the tub. Fill the bathtub about half full of lukewarm or cool water, pouring the bath preparation into the water while it is being drawn. If you are using a homemade herbal-tea bath, strain the preparation into the tub using a tea strainer.

Enter the bathtub nude and immerse yourself completely into the water. It is very important to include your head. Make sure that the bath solution soaks every part of your body. Don't use soap. You should remain in a spiritual bath for at least six to eight minutes, praying (this is important) for it to be effective. When you leave the tub, wrap your hair in a towel, but don't dry it. Put on a bathrobe to cover your wet body, but don't towel dry. Your body should dry in the air.

Following are formulas for the two baths I recommend: the psychic-tension bath, which relieves psychic tension and promotes healing, and the herbal bath.

For the psychic-tension bath, mix together:

> 1/4 cup Epsom salts
> 1 cup bicarbonate of soda (baking soda)
> 1 tablespoon salt (use either sea salt or table salt)

The herbal bath, which is also excellent, is formed by making tea from an herb and using the tea in a bath. In general, use one tablespoon of the herb desired and pour a cup of boiling water over it. Steep until the tea cools to room temperature, then strain out the herb. One cup of tea to half a tub of water is sufficient.

Regular cooking basil is one herb that can be used in a bath. It both protects and cleanses psychic "dirt" and prevents the accumulation of further negative influences. This is good to use when you have to face intimidating people. Another herb that can be used is nutmeg. It has the effect of making people more open to you and removing negative vibrations.

Doing meditation every day, with no desire other than to grow spiritually, will improve your aura and reintegrate it naturally. Also, a strong belief in the power of the will coupled with determination and a strong connection to your spiritual source is your best defense against negative energies. As you grow spiritually and your emotional body becomes clearer, you will become more secure and centered. Then astral invasion will no longer be a problem because you will have healed in you what had been attracting the entities all along.

Psychic development—that is, consciously trying to develop one's psychic abilities—is not a good idea for an alcoholic in the early stages of recovery. In my case, developing myself psychically weakened my sobriety. I became more sensitive to people's negative vibrations, and their negative moods affected me more than before. As I opened up psychically, I became more irritable and depressed. It is possible for the psychic to develop emotional problems because he or she cannot avoid seeing and hearing what is happening on the astral plane.

Psychic development is not spiritual development, which is mandatory for the alcoholic. Spiritual development means becoming more attuned to the God within. It involves growing in love for others, growing in self-awareness, and increasing spiritual knowledge and wisdom, wisdom being the application of knowledge. A person may be very psychic and not at all spiritual. On the other hand, a person can grow spiritually without any psychic development, as such development is not necessary for spiritual advancement.

Alcoholism is primarily a spiritual disease. It is a conflict between the soul and the personality, as explained in chapter 1. Quitting on your own without a spiritual program, such as the twelve-step programs, is dangerous. Spiritual growth is accomplished through meditation and contact with the higher self. For further information on this subject, refer to chapters 9 and 10.

SEVEN

Healing the Physical Body: The Kundalini Fire

The illumination grew brighter and brighter, the roaring louder. I experienced a rocking sensation and then felt myself out of my body, entirely enveloped in a halo of light. . . . I felt the point of consciousness that was myself growing wider surrounded by waves of light. . . . I was now all Consciousness, without any outline, without any idea of corporal appendage, without any feeling or sensation coming from the senses, immersed in a seal of light. . . . I was no longer myself, or to be more accurate, no longer as I knew myself to be, a small point of awareness confined in a body but instead was a vast circle of consciousness in which the body was but a point, bathed in light and in a state of exaltation and happiness impossible to describe.[18]
—Meditation experience described by Gopi Krishna
in *Kundalini: The Evolutionary Energy in Man*

One way or another, people who have issues with alcohol are trying to depress spiritual energy, also known as kundalini energy, the life force of the universe. It is the Christ consciousness, the supreme potential of humans, and, as shakti, it is the female creative force. Kundalini energy exists in every human being, but in some people it is still in a dormant state. When it is awakened, a person's spiritual evolution begins. Kundalini energy will transform and push humanity on to its next evolutionary level.

As kundalini awakens in the human body, it spirals upward, moving through and activating each chakra. The chakras are vortices of energy, a series of seven small force fields extending from the base of the spine to the crown of the head that act as interconnecting links for subtle but powerful energy frequencies in the body. After activating each chakra, kundalini moves out of the body through the crown center at the top of the head.

The process of "kundalini rising" is experienced in many ways. Although there are certain generalities, each person's experience of this phenomenon is unique. The length of time it takes to happen also differs for each person. Kundalini rising may be felt as heat or as a liquid "fire"—especially along the spine or over the top of the head. It may be felt as pressure or tightness, especially near the various chakra areas. A person with rising kundalini may feel dizziness or shakiness. The process may be temporarily fatiguing to the physical body, thus good health is a necessity. The intuition expands. Different states of consciousness, such as bliss and ecstasy, are experienced and intertwined with normal consciousness.

The kundalini fire is more important to the physical body than it might seem. The body is made up not only of flesh and blood but also of subtle energies and *nadis*, channels through which life force is circulated. Just as there are many wires in the engine of a car, similarly within the body there are many nadis. In the physical form, they appear as blood vessels, nerves, and lymph ducts.

These nadis perform different functions. Some are channels for blood, some for mind, some for prana or life energy, and so on. Among the 720 million nadis that make up the human body, there are a hundred that are critically important because they support all the others.

All of our thoughts originate from the central nadi in the brain, and all of our karma and impressions from many lives are also lodged there. When kundalini is awakened, all the past impressions and karma come out. Such memories may make you feel very negative and angry. You shouldn't be afraid if this happens, though, as kundalini is expelling the karma of countless lives.

Psychiatrist Lee Sannella, author of *The Kundalini Experience: Psychosis or Transcendence,* studies kundalini in strictly physiological terms. He bases his theories on case histories of people who have had spontaneous awakenings of kundalini. According to traditional teaching, kundalini ascends from the chakra at the base of the spine, along the central channel, and up to the crown center at the top of the head. Dr. Sannella's clinical observations, as well as those of spiritual teachers Swami Muktananda and Gopi Krishna, indicate that kundalini flows from the feet and legs, along the back of the trunk or along the spine, to the head. From there it flows down over the face and through the throat, terminating in the stomach, or solar-plexus chakra.

On its upward course, kundalini energy activates and energizes the seven chakras, clearing blockages and past karma as it goes. In the process, it encounters all kinds of structural blockages. The main ones are usually located in the base chakra at the anal area, in the heart center, and in the center between the eyebrows (the third eye). Yogis have techniques for removing these blockages or stress points.

Once kundalini clears a blockage, it continues on its upward path until eventually it reaches the crown center at the top of the head. This path is not a straight upward ascent, as the energy may disperse in several directions simultaneously. It becomes focused again, however, once it reaches the crown chakra.

An analogy can be made to a hose. When water flows

with great force through a small rubber hose, it may cause the hose to whip uncontrollably, but when the same amount of water flows through a large fire hose, you may not notice its passage at all. Likewise, when the flow of kundalini through certain stressed or blocked areas of the body and mind meets resistance, it causes turbulence in those areas.

Practitioners of tantric yoga and hatha yoga insist that the only way to guide the awakened kundalini is through the central channel. Only when it is on this path, they say, can people avoid its unpleasant side effects, which range from mild discomfort to insanity.

The knowledge of kundalini is worldwide. Though in the West it is known mostly in esoteric circles, many psychologists, scientists, and physicists are beginning to take a clinical view of it, regarding it as another tool for therapy.

Although people talk about the "awakening" of kundalini, everyone's kundalini is already awake. Kundalini dwells in the center of the body, at the base of the spine, controlling and maintaining the whole physiological system. It is responsible for the body's functioning. Kundalini also allows our minds to think and gives us the power to discriminate and make decisions.

As long as kundalini is "asleep" in the body, a person will be no more than a human being, unable to obtain enlightenment or reach his or her spiritual potential. In many people kundalini has uncoiled up to the waist. But in order to be beneficial for the healing of addictions, it must rise farther.

Prana is a key concept in understanding kundalini. It is the "life breath," the vital force of the body as well as the vital force of the universe. Prana is the force that carries out the different functions of the body in an orderly manner. In modern terminology it would be considered the force that assists in bodily oxygenation and regeneration.

Often, when kundalini first becomes active, a person will

feel heavy-headed and sleepy. This is a result of the movement of prana and is a sign that kundalini has been awakened. By releasing prana, kundalini purifies the body of imbalances and blockages that often cause disease. As kundalini rises up the spinal cord and releases prana, it clears the body of traumas and diseases. But in order for a disease to be expelled, it often must first surface and manifest physically. This is nothing to be alarmed at; the previously hidden trauma or disease is only coming up to be expelled permanently.

Following are different ways in which kundalini can be awakened:

1. Spontaneously, without effort;
2. Consciously, such as with the practice of various yoga exercises;
3. Through repetition of a mantra, a sacred word, or a cosmic sound invested with the power of God.

Some people awaken kundalini consciously, and in these cases kundalini will break the grip of the lower self. However, the most dramatic signs of kundalini awakening are physical and psychological manifestations. As kundalini ascends, you may feel vibrations, tingling, fluttering, or even itching inside the body. You may have headaches or hear voices that seem to be coming from within, and during meditation your body may become temporarily locked into certain yogic postures. You may have visions of bright light and/or faraway scenes. You may feel powerful waves of emotions such as anger, anxiety, sadness, joy, ecstasy, devotion, and cosmic harmony, all of which may tend to dominate your psyche. Your thinking may speed up or slow down, and your thoughts may seem irrational or strange; sometimes when this happens you may feel as if you're going crazy, especially if you have no outside guidance. In time, however, you will learn to integrate all this.

Benefits of Kundalini

The purpose of kundalini awakening is to increase your general vitality and to enable you to dwell in a high state of consciousness. You may also develop abilities like clairvoyance or clairaudience, psychic healing abilities, and even the ability to send kundalini energy to others. However, just because your kundalini is awakened doesn't necessarily mean you will experience all these abilities—sometimes you may experience only one or two. And, of course, dwelling on the development of these powers rather than focusing on your spiritual development would be a mistake, as psychic powers are not the path itself but merely signposts along the way. Treat them with lightness, wisdom, and joy.

I once heard of a Spanish woman who had just emerged from a suicidal depression. She went to see a guru, and he awakened the kundalini in her. No longer suicidal, she felt that at last there was something to live for—that her life now had meaning. Kundalini will heal your addictions, put your life in order, and give your life new meaning.

When awakened kundalini rises through the central channel, it pierces the seven chakras and finally brings about *samadhi*, a transcendental state of awareness in which people experience the supreme reality and become self-realized. In this state we recognize God's presence in all things. However, as *samadhi* is a conscious experience, it makes us more alert and aware while we continue to function in the world. People who have experienced it say they feel blissfully submerged in an ocean full of pure golden consciousness that is impossible to describe.

The closer we come to the inner self, the more happiness we feel. Ordinary activities give us this feeling of happiness. When we wake up from sleep, our minds are quiet and we reflect on our inner contentment. If we used to think happiness was something outside ourselves, we now find that it is inside. Through awakening kundalini, our understanding,

our perception, and our entire beings are gradually transformed. We look upon the world in new way. We are better
able to function in the everyday world. What once may have
seemed difficult and frustrating now seems challenging, and
we are filled with new enthusiasm.

Kundalini energy will take care of you in every way. It
will make you able to look after your family better and take
care of your business or profession more skillfully. It will
make you more of an artist, writer, or inventor. Once it is
awakened, it will release latent creative abilities you didn't
know you had. It will even improve your memory and
concentration.

Fears about Kundalini

Kundalini energy, on its ascent through the central channel, causes physical symptoms when it meets a blockage.
These can cause fear as well as discomfort. One lady had
severe headaches manifesting as her main blockage, but the
pain came from her resistance to the process, not from the
process itself. Once she started to accept the process, the
headaches went away. Similarly, alcoholics often drink because of the physical symptoms of blockage; they do not
know what is really happening. They are more sensitive than
others to the symptoms of kundalini energy.

Once kundalini energies release prana into the system,
there is a profound purification of the emotional, physical,
and spiritual bodies. Jeff Green, in *Uranus: Freedom From the
Known*, wrote about this purification. Following is my interpretation of what he said.

Because the individual is resisting growth, kundalini
seeks out cells that need purification. For example, a woman
is in emotional turmoil over a situation involving the breakup
of a relationship, but she is unaware that she has suppressed
certain past-life memories that have been influencing both
her perception of the situation and her reaction to it. These

suppressed memories are now restricting her growth, and her present emotional states are linked to these past-life experiences. The fact that the same situation comes up over and over again means that this woman has not dealt with and resolved all the issues. Thus they must be relived so that they can be resolved and a new growth phase can occur. This woman should reflect on her feelings to find their deeper meaning and should find someone to share this with—someone she can trust to help her relive and release her emotions. This friend should also help her to objectify what is occurring.

Green believes the action of the planet Uranus stimulates kundalini, causing an increase in pressure on the nerves around the second chakra (located in women between the ovaries and in men about an inch or so below the navel). The second chakra has to do with reproduction and basic sexual drives. Kundalini energy can influence this chakra, causing a person to experience such extremes as an intensification of sexual desire at one point and a total loss of sexual interest at another point.

According to astrology, most people undergo a life crisis between the ages of thirty-eight and forty-two. This is called the Uranus opposition, and kundalini is triggered by Uranus between these ages. Interestingly, there is an increase of alcoholism in people between those same ages. At the Uranus opposition time, kundalini rises up the spine. If the energy is allowed to flow freely without interference, it will unblock each chakra on its own. Alcoholics seem to sense this natural impetus to action and usually drink to keep it down.

Green contends that only a small percentage of people pass through this life crisis successfully. It is a time when we start to feel restless and begin a reexamination of our entire lives. We may come to a realization or conviction that our lives have been based on the ideals and values of our peer groups. We experience a crisis of identity, and we feel a need to discover and define ourselves in new ways. Also, during this time, we reevaluate our goals and life directions. We see the need for change but often lack the courage to break free of conditions or definitions that give us false identities. If this transit is successfully completed, we develop an awareness of who we are not. Then we will want to change our goals— perhaps the entire direction of our lives—in order to fulfill the real purpose of our existences.

Barbara Hand Clow, in her book *Chiron: Rainbow Bridge Between the Inner and Outer Planets*, says that those who fail to resolve the crisis of the Uranus opposition usually experience problems in the heart, the throat, and sometimes the third-eye chakra. Men experience an increase in heart attacks at this age. Women may experience blocks in their throat chakras, resulting in difficulty in speaking and being heard, or the development of laryngitis. The so-called mid-life crisis, at about age forty-two, sets in when we have missed the opportunities to transform ourselves at the Uranus opposition. Alcoholics feel this crisis deeply. Often, instead of facing their issues, they retreat to the bottle, hoping their problems will vanish. They suppress their pain, carrying on their lives in a kind of stoic resignation. On the other hand, if we transform ourselves at the Uranus opposition and are able to integrate our issues, kundalini energy will balance in our bodies and all our chakras will open.

The main problem with a spontaneous kundalini awakening is that alcoholics are either frightened by, or resist and judge, the altered states it produces. They focus on its negative effects. An alcoholic may comment, "My body is dissolving, I am tingling. I am burning up. The sounds are too loud." Each time people resist these sensations, they are trapped by them, and fear and misunderstanding cause them to struggle. However, they can learn to enjoy these sensations as natural occurrences.

If you feel kundalini rising too rapidly and intensely, Dr.

Sannella's advice is to slow the process down by eating more and by focusing on basic grounding activities such as taking showers, jogging, walking, digging in the garden—anything that connects with the Earth. Bodywork and massage are also helpful, and acupuncture works well for heavy kundalini energies, especially if it is done by someone who knows how to balance the nadi system along with doing the acupuncture.

When your chakras open, you will feel a variety of physical symptoms. When the throat chakra opens, there may be tension and coughing. The opening of the lower chakras may bring tension and fear; there can be nausea and release through vomiting. The opening of the sexual chakra can bring difficulties in controlling the sex drive. When the heart chakra opens you may feel love and compassion, although this opening is usually painful, as most of us have bands of constriction holding tension over our hearts.

One of the bigger problems in the case of spontaneous kundalini awakening is a fear of going insane, as people often do not know how to interpret their symptoms. Not knowing or being aware of the deeper spiritual possibilities of kundalini, and lacking a background in esoteric philosophy, addicts panic over some of the more dramatic symptoms. Dr. Sannella says that the psychological problems may resemble schizophrenia and probably would be diagnosed as such by a physician.

Gopi Krishna had many problems with his kundalini awakening, but knew enough not to consult a psychiatrist. He knew that professional counseling, whether medical or psychological, was an unequal relationship wherein the professional considered himself or herself to have superior views.

Remember, a spontaneous kundalini awakening is a blessing, not a curse. If you feel you may be experiencing a kundalini problem, it is best to consult someone with experience in this area. It is important to understand that the kundalini process is neither insane nor psychotic. True, your experiences may not be "normal" in the usual sense of the word, but they are probably not disorganized enough to be considered psychotic. Receiving negative criticism of your condition may undermine your self-confidence, so trust your process.

After a kundalini awakening, your nervous system will become more sensitive, and you should pay more attention to your diet. In time, however, you will integrate your new experiences into your daily life and will be able to function effectively.

Dr. Sannella further writes that those who have the most problems with the kundalini process are natural psychics. The experience is more intense for them; this is necessary to give them the knowledge they need and to build up their self-confidence.

Christina Grof, herself a recovering alcoholic, said she used alcohol to suppress kundalini. Her kundalini was chaotic and unpredictable and would act up at the most inappropriate times. For example, she developed an intense craving for sweets. As explained in chapter 11, all alcoholics are hypoglycemic; they crave sugar intensely and use alcohol to satisfy that craving, but, as Grof says, kundalini and alcohol make a very dangerous combination.

Grof founded the Spiritual Emergency Network (SEN) in 1980 in Menlo Park, California, as a grass-roots response to the need for information, recognition, and support for those undergoing spiritual crisis. Too often, she found, those undergoing such a crisis are labeled psychotic and locked up in hospital mental wards instead of getting the kind of assistance they really need.

Learning to recognize these spiritual crisis states is imperative. SEN offers advice on the telephone to people experiencing any sort of spiritual emergency, and many people call after experiencing kundalini rising spontaneously. It also offers an information-and-referral service with education and a training program. The telephone number of the network is (415) 327-2776.

Gopi Krishna was an Indian railroad official who in 1937 experienced a spontaneous kundalini awakening. Energy began dancing and coursing powerfully through his body, but his wonderment and bliss soon faded. The electrical energy changed directions and went up the Pingala nerve, which is located on the right side of the spine; it is the nerve that regulates the flow of heat in the body. He became somewhat incapacitated, as the energy would not stop, leaving him tormented and sleepless for days on end. Only after twelve years of this frustrating experience was he able to integrate the energies in his body and use them in a creative way as the author of a dozen books. Then in 1943 he had another powerful kundalini experience, culminating in ecstatic unification, or *samadhi.*

According to Gopi Krishna, kundalini is the basis of all mysticism. There is every reason to believe that mysticism, transcendental knowledge, and even genius can come naturally to any person, as it is part of the evolutionary mechanism underlying all spiritual and psychic phenomena. But how can we account for the absence of physical symptoms in mystics? The first explanation is that these people are free of the blockages that make the process more complicated for others such as alcoholics. The second view is that mystics have experienced only a partial kundalini awakening. Both positions have their supporters, and further research is clearly needed. It has been said that one ecstatic experience can change an entire lifetime. As addicts we should be striving for such an experience.

Dr. Sannella cautions that any practice designed to speed up the kundalini process, such as the breath-control exercises known as *pranayama,* are dangerous unless practiced under the guidance of a guru, preferably one who has completed the entire kundalini process himself or herself. Yoga breath techniques should not be initiated alone, as they can unleash strong, subtle energies that a person might not know how to handle.

Hatha yoga is another system used to awaken kundalini. It uses an elaborate system of postures for maintaining physical health as well as for spiritual development. The exercises in this book may also trigger kundalini, as might any psychic exercise. The idea is to raise kundalini gently, in order to break the grip of the addicted lower self. The electrical energy purifies the lower body and reduces the desire for alcohol. Acupuncture can be used to assist the balance and flow of body energies during the process.

EIGHT

Clearing the Emotional Body

Alcoholics must use a system of emotional release consistently and continually. Otherwise, their emotions can build up to toxic levels, resulting in overreaction and even drinking relapses.

There are areas on the Earth's surface that provide release from negative emotional states. I used to notice that whenever I was near a body of water or a mountain, I would feel better. These areas generate negative ions, which neutralize our emotional states. Immersing the body in water also releases static electricity, which in turn affects the nervous system. Look for natural healing spots such as vortices (places on Earth that respond to galactic energy), which contain the higher-frequency energy that is so nourishing to the emotional body.

For some time each day, I go to a place where I can be alone. There, I review my feelings and concerns and what I have learned from my experiences. I do the "Observer Self" exercise explained in the Appendix. This allows me to detach myself emotionally. I also review my relationships to see if others are throwing me off balance. This is the key to establishing control.

Sooner or later, every alcoholic must come to terms with his or her past. It is possible to redefine the past in terms of your present consciousness. Everything that has happened has been for a reason, and only in retrospect can you understand that reason. When you look back at your past experiences, you will see that, given the choices you had, you made the perfect choice in each instance. True, with the knowledge you now have you may have chosen differently, but you did the best you could at the time.

Attribute meaning to your past. Review your experiences in a nonjudgmental way; forgive yourself and others. Being stuck in the past is self-defeating. Assimilate from your past the lessons you have learned and get on with your life. Otherwise you will have huge uncleared parts of yourself that may compel you to drink.

Evolution is a choice. We can choose to not evolve, but if even one small part of us is awakened, it provides a tension that stimulates us toward growth. Often we feel a deep dissatisfaction with a nongrowth orientation, and this can be a stimulus in itself.

As alcoholics, we must make a continual effort to release our emotions. Often we become so identified with our emotional bodies that we think we *are* our feeling states. To have an intellectual understanding of emotional release is not enough. Intellectually we may know we shouldn't be angry, but our emotional bodies need to get the message, too. We must experience these mental concepts at all levels of our beings—physical, emotional, and mental—before they can be totally released and fade out of consciousness.

In many cases it works like this: We have a mental insight with what appears to be an emotional catharsis. We feel as if the emotion has been released. Then, a few days later, a similar emotion-provoking situation occurs, and again we get a nervous stomach. What happened? We have only partially released the emotion; our cells still haven't gotten the message. We could worsen the situation by thinking less of ourselves for taking so long to release the emotion, but this attitude will not help us. It means that we have not completely understood the nature and purpose of the particular problem.

The problem lies in the unconscious mind. Some people can release emotions through past-life therapy, which often works when other types of therapy fail. Barbara Hand Clow and Chris Griscom are two who have used past-life regression successfully. Few of us have much awareness of what is buried in our subconscious. Emotions can arise and overwhelm us at almost any time, but if these emotions are coaxed up and lifted out with understanding and compassion, in time they will lessen. Some emotions have strong energies attached to them and may require the help of a competent therapist in order to be released.

The biggest problem we have as alcoholics is dealing with guilt and the consciousness of being a "victim." There is no such thing as victimhood. Victim consciousness is a false belief. It is the belief that being the *effect* of events is beyond our control. None of us is innocent. All present-day victims have been victimizers in past lifetimes. As Chris Griscom says:

> There are those out there who deserve the judgment because they did it wrong. I know that this is a tremendously difficult concept to accept, but other people didn't do anything that you didn't allow them to do. It is impossible from a cosmic perspective for it to happen any other way. Impossible.[19]

We say that we don't want to be a victim any more. Yet, we must have some attachment to the role, or we wouldn't keep attracting it over and over. What are we getting out of it? What lesson are we not learning? To solve the victim dilemma, we must ask, "What is the soul purpose of this trial?" This book offers some clues.

Victim consciousness makes no sense from the viewpoint of the personality, but from a higher perspective it does. We choose to be victims over and over. We are responsible for all our actions. To solve the dilemma, we must each clean up our own act.

Is there any abuse in your life? Think about it. We draw lessons such as abuse to ourselves in order to teach us, but often we just spin the same circles over and over, without learning from the experiences. Those who have been victims have often been abusers in the same lifetimes. In order to erase the karmic blueprint—the plan of the soul for all karmic obligations—we must heal ourselves of this tendency once and for all. (For more information on clearing the karmic blueprint, read Chris Griscom's *Ecstasy Is a New Frequency*.)

Another manifestation of victim consciousness is passivity. Psychologists have long known that passivity promotes disease and distorts creative energy. When passivity becomes crystallized, it turns to self-hatred and promotes a feeling of powerlessness.

The beautiful thing about the Observer Self Meditation (see Appendix) is that you can create a new reality with it. You will discover in many instances that you *do* have a choice about your reality; that you are separate from your feeling states; that you can consciously manipulate your affairs; and that you are not a victim of circumstances. Observing all this with a quiet mind will help you to decide creatively what you can do in any given situation. The goal is to reach a point where you can observe yourself at the same time that you are feeling or acting.

The observer-self consciousness must be experienced in order to be understood. As it becomes a part of your life, it gradually changes your consciousness. At first you may think you are a poor observer, for you may be caught up in emotional turmoil. Be patient; in time you will get better. The technique may take several years to perfect, but gradually you will see that you are separate from the conditions surrounding you. You will come to realize that no matter how bad those conditions have been, you still remain, and that it is your self that truly matters. In time you will also see that you can choose your own level of involvement in the conditions of your life. With the Observer Self Meditation, you will gradually learn to accept life as it is and yourself as you are.

Before closing this chapter, I would like to mention some grounding and centering techniques. The Rainbow Bridge Meditation described in chapter 10 will ground and center you to some extent. From this meditation you may get a kundalini-rising effect. If you do, there is nothing to fear. It is a very pleasant experience. The techniques that follow are for those of you not using the Rainbow Bridge Meditation.

The first technique involves centering yourself with your breath. To be centered means to be just yourself. Rather than judging yourself as being this or that, it is a feeling of "being here now," which is an experience apart from thought. When you are centered, you feel collected rather than scattered. It is a state of calm receptivity. When you are relaxed and your mind is clear, then you can center your awareness. Begin by breathing slowly. Then, as you exhale, imagine that you are breathing out through a spot an inch or so below your navel. You may want to center yourself by repeating the word "center" or by using a special number or color that brings you to a centering point. Breath changes your vibration: slower, deeper breathing moves you into a calmer, more centered space. Once this control is achieved, you will no longer be at the mercy of your emotions or your environment.

There are several exercises that promote "grounding." Grounding creates a secure attachment and connection between yourself and the Earth. It permits the energy from the Earth to flow through the soles of your feet and into your body. When you are not grounded, you feel nervous, spaced out, hyperactive, and often less effective in your daily life.

There are many methods of grounding yourself. One is

to carry iron crystals with you. Iron pyrite is extremely grounding. Another method is to imagine roots growing out of your feet as you walk barefoot on the ground. Or try the following technique:

1. Sit still with a straight spine and center yourself.
2. Imagine a gold cord of light leaving the bottom of your spine and traveling down into the center of the Earth. If you are indoors, envision the cord of light going through the floor and then into the Earth.
3. Use your breathing to send increasing amounts of energy through the golden cord and even farther toward the center of the Earth. You may begin to feel heavier, as if your body has expanded.
4. If you feel any tenseness or stiffness, imagine each exhalation releasing these blockages.
5. Continue this exercise for at least three minutes or until you feel grounded.

Clearing the Chakras

Cleansing and clearing the chakras is a powerful healing exercise that we can all do for ourselves. You may have to do the exercise four or five times before you get a clearing.

All of the energy bodies or levels of consciousness are intertwined and joined together at the chakras, which may be seen psychically as swirling vortices along the spinal cord and in the head. Each chakra vibrates at a different rate. Cosmic energy in the form of light rays is pulled into the body through the chakras and distributed along the spine so that it flows throughout the entire body. When this energy is absorbed into the body and is able to flow uninterrupted, the body is in balance and therefore healthy. If for any reason this harmonious flow is disturbed, however, difficulties arise. Each chakra has different qualities. If there is a lack or a surplus of a particular quality, an imbalance occurs and the flow of energy is disrupted.

Alcoholics often have problems with grounding and centering, so if the following exercise is done correctly, it is profoundly healing. First, try to get a feel for your chakras. By focusing on each chakra, you can become aware of the flow of energy throughout your being and take note of any disruptions. Try to sense where your chakras are; you'll locate them with a little practice. Once you can do that, you'll want to clean them.

Your chakras can become blocked by your unexpressed emotions or by your clinging to attitudes, feelings, and beliefs that are no longer useful to you and therefore have become a drain on your energy. This technique enables you to psychically remove anything that doesn't belong in your chakras.

Following are the locations and specific functions of each of the seven chakras.

1. The first chakra, called the base, or root, chakra, is located at the base of the spine and has to do with the ability to survive and to make changes. Blockages here can result in poor grounding and insecurity, with a resultant focus on survival.

2. The second chakra is located between the ovaries in women and an inch or so below the navel in men. It has to do with reproduction and sexuality. If you have an excess of energy here, you may become too sensitive to other people. If this chakra is too open, you will absorb or become overattached to other people's feelings and become drained. You may have difficulty determining what energy is coming from you and what is coming from other people. It is better to learn to connect with people from the heart chakra, as it is far less draining.

3. The third chakra is located in the solar plexus, which is about an inch or so above the navel. This chakra has to do with how you maintain and create balance within yourself. This is the center that governs your

self-esteem and self-confidence. Blockages here can create a lack of emotional balance and self-confidence.

4. The fourth center is the heart chakra, located in the area of the actual physical heart. Not enough energy here can leave you feeling out of touch. Too much energy here will make you overly sympathetic and anxious; you might also manifest a "savior complex." When this chakra is balanced, you will see clearly where your emotions are springing from. Blockages here can create relationship problems and difficulty in giving or receiving love. Clearing a blockage here will increase your capacity for love. The heart chakra also connects to the insides of the arms and hands, which are known as the healing channels. As you clean this chakra, make sure you are adequately grounded.

5. The fifth, or throat, chakra is located at the base of the skull. It relates to the glands and emotionally to communication. This chakra functions as a connecting bridge between the four lower chakras and the two upper ones. It is the center for the development of clairaudience. This is a dangerous ability to develop unless you are a very emotionally stable person. Opening the throat chakra releases the creative energies, the creative word.

6. The sixth center is the brow chakra, located between the eyebrows. It is also known as the "third eye." This is the space where conscious and unconscious knowledge join. It is the center where you connect with your higher self, and it has to do with mental clarity and intuitive communication. Blockages in this area can create mental confusion, obsessiveness, or difficulty in handling psychic input.

7. The seventh, or crown, chakra is located at the top of the head. This is the center that connects you to a space of pure knowing and intuition. This is where

you connect with your higher self. Blockages here can lead to spiritual lows, resulting in a lack of connectedness to the universe.

In addition to these chakras, there are four secondary chakras—one in each of the hands and feet. The chakras in the feet have to do with the movements you make in life, the path you travel, and your work. If these chakras are blocked, you may have difficulty staying grounded. The hand chakras have to do with creativity and self-expression. Blockages in the energy here can indicate problems with manipulation (either allowing yourself to be manipulated or acting in a manipulative way toward others) and/or problems with the ability to get a grasp on things.

To cleanse and clear the chakras, it is important to relax, ground, and protect yourself. Surround yourself with a white light that permeates your aura. Now visualize your chakras one at a time and notice what, if anything, is blocking them. Remove the blockages by visualizing your hand reaching in and removing the unwanted "stuff," or imagine the stuff draining away.

Don't forget to ground yourself before beginning this exercise. Start with the bottom chakra and work up. After finishing the cleansing, go back and "stabilize" the chakras by merely holding a hand in front of each of them for a moment or two, as if you were trying to get it to stay in place. Touch the ground after the healing exercise. For further information, one of the best books on chakras is *Wheels of Life: A User's Guide to the Chakra System,* by Anodea Judith.

NINE

Contacting the Higher Self

It has been said that reaching the depths of life bereft of spirituality, as we do in alcoholism, opens us up to the possibility of truly spiritual life. A door is opened, and the resulting connection with the higher self brings in healing energy.

I usually contact my higher self through meditation. I believe this is a must for all recovering alcoholics. Meditation grounds and centers us. It is the door to initiation.

As I mentioned earlier, I first contacted my higher self in 1962 through an expansion of consciousness that transformed my life. For you, however, the first contact with your higher self may be quite different. It will reflect the degree of your doubts, your sense of separation, and your feelings of guilt and judgment. When you first try to make contact, all you may get is a triangle or a color. That's OK; just surrender to it, and it will heal you. Trust it, ask it to guide you, and it will. The answers are all within.

Your Personal Altar

To contact your higher self, you have to keep your energy up. Go away by yourself to a quiet spot where you won't be disturbed. You might want to set up an altar that will be there whenever you need a place to attune to higher energies.

Having your own space set aside for meditation is very important.

You might like an amethyst-crystal altar. Amethyst is traditional as a remedy against alcoholism. This beautiful stone has the capacity to bring in spiritual energy, and to support the process of transforming old beliefs and thought patterns. It can balance the energy in your body and make you better able to benefit from meditation. If you can't afford an amethyst-crystal altar, you might keep an amethyst placed on top of your altar, where it will attract healing energy for you.

Go to your altar at the beginning of each day. Refresh yourself through silence and nature, which will revitalize your inner self. Visualize the day ahead of you. See the people you will be dealing with responding to you positively. See your body healthy. See yourself calm and serene, in control of every situation. Release any emotional problems from the previous day, and take time to feel the inner you.

Signs of the Higher Self

By disciplining your subconscious mind, you will permit the energy of your higher self to flow. At first you may sense that your higher self is not there, as you will not be able to touch, feel, hear, or see it. But in a subtle way it is present, and you can see it working in your life. Once you have disciplined your mind and controlled your emotions, the energy of your higher self will flow through you. The more it does, the more light you will have.

You have a responsibility to maintain this balance in your thoughts, in your emotions, and in your physical body. If you don't do this, you may find yourself in an energy pattern that is out of control and can lead to addiction. Once you accept true spiritual responsibility, loving yourself will come more easily, for you will understand that it is *you* who controls your life. Then, once you feel that you can control the present, you are ready to deal with the past.

The transference from reliance on an external god to connection with your higher self is not easy. Alcohol can influence your emotions and cloud your thinking processes, leaving you stuck in your emotional body for up to eighteen months after your last drink.

Sometimes when you think you are reaching your higher self, you may actually be contacting an astral thoughtform instead. But with time and perseverance, you will be able to tell the difference and succeed. Following are some signs that you are definitely being guided by your higher self:

1. Fear is transformed into courage. Fear is an ego mechanism and an illusion. You may fear that you will fail, but you transmute the fear with your will. You acknowledge that you have certain weaknesses, assess your strengths and shortcomings, and have the courage to be what you want to be rather than what others want you to be.
2. Self-pity and blame are transformed into responsibility. No one is to blame. You are testing out life's experiences, and you make mistakes at times. There are no victims. You are totally responsible for the people you attract. By making a choice, you set a chain of events into motion. You consciously create your own reality. Each experience is something you need.
3. Self-absorption is transformed into an aspiration to serve humanity. Feeling a connectedness to others, you discover joy in serving them, which in turn is self-nourishing.
4. Exaggerated mood swings are transformed into serenity. Your mood swings help you to understand your humanness. When your self-esteem gets low, you remember who you are and step out of your self-centeredness. You seek balance in all your emotions.

5. Fragmented knowledge is transformed into holistic truth. Most of the scientific knowledge we have today consists of fragmented knowledge—partial truths. We rarely get the whole picture, which involves using both sides of our brain. The more you become your higher self, the more of your total brain power you use.

6. Role-playing is transformed into an expression of your authentic nature. We play roles because we don't know who we are. Later on we see the roles for what they are. After being on the path, you find out who you are, and you are not afraid to show this self to another. Your desire for external things is transmuted into a quest for self-knowledge. On the way to finding your true identity, you lose interest in using things to satisfy your sense of identity. Self-knowledge leads to a strong identity.

7. Passion is transformed into compassion. You turn inward to look for the truth inside yourself. When you do this, you begin to perceive yourself in a non-judgmental way. This is the way to self-acceptance. It is our judgment of ourselves that holds us back. Once you realize that life is hard, you can see how you've gotten where you are and what price you've had to pay to reach a deeper understanding of the difficulties you've had to pass through. Then you develop compassion for yourself. This compassion you have for yourself then flows out onto others.

8. Powerlessness is transformed into self-mastery. Once you feel that you have the power to choose, and to change what you want, feelings of fear and impotence are overcome.

Don't rely on a recovery program to provide all the answers; this would be a symptom of the disease. Look within to find your answers, and listen to your own intuition, which is the voice of your soul. However, intuitive knowledge can be interpreted wrongly because of your own misperception.

When you get an answer from your higher self, it may not seem like the right answer because you may not be emotionally ready for it. Following are some signs that you are being guided by your intuition:

1. You feel certain that you are headed on the right course. This course may be painful because sometimes it will mean letting go of someone or something that is close to you.
2. The truth of the insight will not contradict other important truths or beliefs you currently hold.
3. The intuitive insight is a flowing feeling rather than a forced feeling.
4. The intuitive insight often comes in the form of symbols requiring interpretation, but not in a literal sense. Once I felt that I was present at the physical death of a personal friend lying in a hospital bed. This did not symbolize the death of my friend, but only an aspect of our relationship that was falling away.

TEN

Meditation Techniques

As mentioned previously, meditation is a powerful way to reach the higher self and form a more permanent identity. There comes a time in the life of every person when further spiritual progress depends upon it. It is literally the footpath of the gods. Following are two meditation programs that I have found to be particularly effective.

The Rainbow Bridge Program

The Rainbow Bridge is a do-it-yourself program to rid the soul of accumulated karma and old thoughtforms. It includes techniques that apply to all levels of the personality. The rationale of the authors of this program is that if we don't clean up our personalities first, then meditation will only tend to reflect our negativity.

The Rainbow Bridge techniques will stimulate fresh insights for you about ways in which you have been emotionally blocked. Your higher self shows you what methods you need to use, and your soul suggests the problems that are inhibiting your growth.

This program is not for everyone, and there are certain built-in convictions that you must have in order to benefit from it. These are more fully explained in the book *Rainbow Bridge*, by Two Disciples[20], but they include the following:

1. A belief that life continues to go on after death, and that we as beings have consciousness;
2. An acknowledgment that life has a purpose entirely different from that which conventional wisdom maintains, and that there is something higher in life that is worth striving for;
3. The conviction that there is a way to reach this state of higher consciousness;
4. A belief that we are responsible for our own reality—that we created it through our own thoughts, feelings, and actions;
5. The realization that there are some who have been successful in reaching this higher consciousness;
6. A recognition that some people have acquired all that is possible to be known during the course of human evolution, and that these beings can serve as guides;
7. A personal responsibility for reaching the goal, no matter what obstacles may stand in the way;
8. A strong desire for a life of service to others.

This program is the fruit of years of research by two anonymous investigators who tried different techniques to see what would work best. The researchers claim that this program brings about profound and permanent changes in people's awareness and energy levels.

There is a mantra that is said before doing the procedures:

> *I am the Soul*
> *I am the Light Divine*
> *I am Love*
> *I am Will*
> *I am Fixed Design*

Members of the Rainbow Bridge can be of any faith or denomination and are asked only to give the techniques a fair try and let their own experience and common sense be their guides.

This program includes special techniques for transforming negative emotions, thoughts, and behavior patterns into their positive counterparts. It is too hard to contact the higher self when our emotions are muddied and our "receiving stations" are not able to respond to higher vibrations. In these situations, our negative thoughtforms and personality patterns have become the inner causes of our anxieties and compulsive behavior patterns. These negative patterns tend to cause disease at some level and cloud our perceptions.

The first part of the work consists of constructing a "central channel" (a column of light that runs through the body). Higher energy is then utilized by the "soul star," a sphere of light that is visualized just above the head to represent the soul. Next, a vortex is used to sweep the aura clean. This vortex resembles a tornado of light. After thus cleansing yourself, you feel more secure that your aura will not collect all the psychic pollution caused by your daily contacts with people and the environment.

The two researchers found that their work was successful to some degree with everyone. Some of the permanent benefits of this program are the following:

1. Exaggerated emotional response is eliminated.
2. The low vibration that makes you vulnerable to infection is absorbed.
3. The techniques for psychic development, yoga, and magic are no longer dangerous for you.
4. Suggestions of self-deprecation and failure are no longer activated.
5. You become more centered and relaxed even during the first six months.
6. You experience more emotional stability and self-control, and you grow in your ability to solve problems, think abstractly, and make decisions.

A second phase of this work is geared toward the breaking up of old thoughtforms and the destruction of them with soul energy. Karma can be cleared without living it out.

Personally, I have used these techniques to maintain quality sobriety, and they have worked very well for me. My perceptions are much clearer and less clouded by my emotions. For more information on Rainbow Bridge, write to The Triune Foundation, P.O. Box 226, Escondido, CA 92025.

Nature of the Soul Course

Another new and effective presentation of ancient wisdom is described in *The Nature of the Soul,* by Lucille Cedercrans. Through the use of meditations, this program aims at putting you in touch with your higher self. The course is broken into three parts: (1) "Who Am I?"; (2) "Why Am I Here?"; and (3) "Techniques for Service to Humanity." The lessons assist in character building and the development of creativity, bringing about an expansion of consciousness. The course takes a year to complete.

These meditations will show you what your faults are and what your motivations are. One of them showed me the entire contents of my subconscious mind. I recommend that this course be taken after one-and-a-half years of sobriety. It is the equivalent of AA's fourth step. Through meditation you will be raising the vibration of your energy field to divine frequency, thus opening the way for healing to move through every atom of your being.

ELEVEN

Elements of Sobriety

This chapter outlines the elements of sobriety: what it takes to stay sober and what things you can do to support yourself in that endeavor. You can work with these elements along with a twelve-step program or some other program, but it is very important to use a support group, as this is the only way the work will be effective. (The types of support groups are covered in chapter 3.) Remember, you have the power to heal yourself, and the more you identify with your higher self, the sooner your healing will take place.

The desire to quit drinking permanently follows on the heels of a conviction that your present existence is futile— that there has to be a better way. With this deep desire to change, no matter what the cost, a corner has been turned and there is no looking back.

Motivation for an alcoholic is extremely important. This motivation must be unconscious as well as conscious. While we are still suffering from the mental and physical pains of drinking, we may intellectually agree to quit. But, after quitting, as the memory of the pain lessens, we may return to drinking because we never accepted the situation at a subconscious level. Surrender involves the acceptance of our drinking problem at two levels: the conscious and the unconscious. Without this motivation, we will not stay sober for long.

Alcohol Withdrawal

There are excellent books on the subject of alcohol withdrawal. The one I recommend most is *The Hidden Addiction* by Janice Phelps, M.D., and Alan Nourse, which discusses how to ease the pain of withdrawal. She suggests that, early in recovery, you be checked for hypoglycemia; it is almost always there. It is better to correct this imbalance as soon as possible, as it will make you tense and irritable. Dr. Phelps recommends doses of five hundred to one thousand milligrams of glutamine (an animo acid) four times a day.

Nutritional Needs

Alcoholics trying to stay sober often become sugar addicts. We crave sugar the way we once craved alcohol, and it can make us just as moody, unstable, and exhausted as when we were drinking. There are some who even maintain that if we keep eating processed sugar, we will eventually return to the bottle.

Dr. E.M. Abramson, who wrote *Body, Mind, and Sugar,* is of this opinion. He says that our bodies are equipped to handle an occasional stress in the form of excess sugar. In these occasional instances, the pancreas produces insulin, which is released into the bloodstream where it destroys the excess sugar. But if we continuously bombard our systems with a large amount of easily absorbed sugar, our self-regulating mechanism becomes damaged and even destroyed. When insulin is released into the bloodstream to counteract a high sugar level, it quickly drops that level far below normal. Then heart and muscle performance weaken; brain and nerve performance are damaged; energy and endurance levels fall drastically; and emotional stability and control disappear. At this point we crave a quick pickup from sugar, coffee, or certain drugs that will quickly relieve the symptoms. But the relief is only temporary. Once again the pancreas overreacts to this new onslaught of sugar, and again it overproduces the insulin. It is a vicious cycle: we are happy and energetic when the sugar level is high, and totally exhausted, confused, and stressed a few hours later. I recommend that sugar be eliminated as soon as possible from the diet of every alcoholic. If this seems to be too much for you in your early recovery, begin with a certain intake and then initiate a gradual cutback until your sugar intake is eliminated altogether.

Many people also have the belief that once they stop drinking, their nutritional deficiencies will be resolved and their bodies will return to a healthy state. In reality, the opposite is true. Our nutritional needs remain critical long after we stop abusing drugs and alcohol. For complete information on nutrition, refer to *The Hidden Addiction* by Janice Phelps, M.D., and Alan Nourse or *Staying Sober: A Nutrition and Exercise Program for the Recovering Alcoholic* by Judy Myers.

Avoid fad diets, especially ones using massive doses of vitamins. A well-balanced diet is extremely important. Alcoholics don't metabolize vitamins properly while they are drinking, so even a recovering alcoholic who is overweight has a malnutrition problem.

It is also desirable to take L-glutamine, an animo acid available in health-food stores. This will help soothe away the irritability that goes along with alcohol withdrawal. Go easy on meat, too—a badly damaged liver cannot handle the high level of animo acids from too much protein. Eat plenty of fresh fruit and vegetables, and milk products. Excessive coffee, unless decaffeinated, should be avoided. Food also should be attractively served, as recovering alcoholics often lack appetites.

According to the new schools of nutrition, the healthiest diet is one that concentrates on whole-grain breads, cereals, and pastas, and beans, fresh fruits, and fresh vegetables—the so-called "complex carbohydrates." These are low in fat and sodium (salt) and high in important vitamins, minerals, and fiber. That may be why so many people find that they feel better, both physically and emotionally, when they switch from a diet of sugar-laden, overly processed foods to one that emphasizes complex carbohydrate snacks in between meals.

Doctors also recommend that to avoid blood-sugar problems, you should eat several smaller meals per day instead of the usual three big meals. Or they suggest that you moderate the traditional meal plan by eating smaller portions at the table and then having high-protein or complex-carbohydrate snacks between meals.

Not everyone suffering from the vague collection of hypoglycemia symptoms may be hypoglycemic. The truth is, hypoglycemia is a very controversial issue in medical circles. Many physicians contend that it is a rare problem—hardly the epidemic we are often led to believe. Others, however, cautiously point out that while extreme cases are uncommon, low blood sugar may affect all of us to some degree.

Alcoholics sometimes develop thiamine (vitamin B_1) deficiencies and have problems with short-term memory loss. They may remember in detail that little cafe in Paris twenty years ago but not what they had for supper the previous night. They also have increased needs for vitamins B, B_{12}, and C, copper, calcium, zinc, potassium, and magnesium.

Many nutritional diseases in alcoholics are treatable with vitamin therapy prescribed by a physician after a specific diagnosis. Wernicke-Korsakoff syndrome and beriberi are diseases that respond to the vitamin-B complex. Wernicke-Korsakoff syndrome is a form of psychosis caused by damage to the nervous system from excessive drinking and vitamin deficiencies.

Selfishness

Selfishness is an important part of any recovery program, at least in the beginning. We have to have a strong sense of self before we can give to others. Our ego needs are important. We drank because these needs were not satisfied. Recovery involves putting our sobriety first—before our jobs, our mates, or even our children. This means that we must be willing to leave a relationship if that relationship threatens our sobriety. This rule must be followed in the beginning.

Resentment and Guilt

Resentment is closely allied with guilt. When we don't live up to other people's expectations, we feel a vague sense of guilt as resentment for their power over us. Alcoholics have a very hard time with both guilt and resentment, and both have to be lifted before any permanent sobriety can ensue.

Healing Crisis

It is important to understand the concept of a "healing crisis" in tackling such problems as resentment, guilt, and grief. When we begin to look at a problem honestly, it may flare up, stirring up the emotions we are trying to heal. This is normal—it is called a healing crisis. Temporarily we may feel worse, but it is the beginning of getting better. Experiencing the problem anew and seeing where it comes from is part of the healing process.

Pain

As alcoholics, we must come to terms with our pain. There is no way to get through life without a lot of suffering, and alcoholics almost all drink to avoid pain. A spirit by the name of Hilarion, writing through medium Mabel Collins, says:

We have the instinctive desire to relieve pain, but we work in externals in this as in everything else. We simply alleviate it; and if we do more, and drive it from its first chosen stronghold, it reappears in some other place with reinforced vigor. If it is eventually driven off the physical plane by persistent and successful effort, it reappears on the mental or emotional planes where no man can touch it. . . . In intense pain a point is reached where it is indistinguishable from the opposite, pleasure. This is indeed so, but few have the heroism or the strength to suffer to such a far point.[21]

We drank when we felt overwhelmed. We used these feelings to justify our addictions. As Chris Griscom puts it:

We choose to be overwhelmed, choose to be defenseless, and it is imprinted and crystallized in the mind. The mind, then, continues to make sure that the emotional body activates it, so it begins again. "I am bad, I am helpless, I can't."[22]

Alcoholics have a strong death wish. Some feel ambivalent about living and anger at having to be here, as well as a lack of acceptance of life itself. In order to live fully, we have to resolve our ambivalence about life and death.

We cannot always assume that once we have some years of sobriety our death wish has been transformed. This is often not the case. Even an unconscious death wish can create a reality we don't want—including negative conditions, emotional shocks, and traumatic events leading to feelings of hopelessness and despair. The first thing to do is to accept the fact that we have a death wish and accept responsibility for it. From there, we can decide what life means to us and whether we wish to stay. If we decide that life is worth living, we can develop a strong desire to be healed.

Often, in our efforts to avoid pain, we fail to get the message of the pain, and believe me, there is always a message. Look at the pain and ask, "What is the meaning of this? What is it telling me?" There is often more pain in sobriety than in drinking. The irritability and depression we go through while in withdrawal is often worse than the pain we drank to escape from. During the first year of sobriety, mood swings often occur because of the withdrawal of alcohol from the body cells. Pain is something we have to come to terms with.

There will be setbacks and "dark nights of the soul" along the way—times when you feel you are facing the insurmountable and maybe even times when you feel you are dying. I cannot promise that it won't be painful, but I can promise that you will get through it if you surrender.

Surrender

Surrender is the most essential element of sobriety. It has nothing to do with giving up your power to an external god. Surrender is turning your life over to the real self that dwells within. It means giving up perceiving the world from an ego perspective. It is turning your life over to the real self that you've always been, letting go of your ego-limited viewpoint—getting the whole picture.

The process of surrender contains the following steps:

1. Being aware of the illusions in which you are immersed;
2. Desiring to know the truth and opening yourself to this truth as it manifests itself;
3. Remaining open to the truth, even if it becomes very painful;
4. Having the courage that will make you desire to see the truth as it really is, without its rose coloring.

Surrender is an essential part of any recovery program. It is analogous to the third step of AA.

On looking back, I see that conditions and obstacles I perceived as blocks to my progress were chances to test the principle of truth that led to an expansion of consciousness. The old life dies so that a new one can be born.

My first mystical experience at age twenty-two came after my acceptance of a situation that was very heartbreaking to me. (We all get lazy and complacent, even in regard to living with pain.) Lately I have experienced situations that have tested my faith. After surrendering to them I felt renewed; peace and joy returned. Recovery means dying to the ego-defined viewpoint and surrendering to the higher self.

Resistance

Force does not become creative until it meets resistance. We often use resistance to slow down or postpone our evolution. We feel we are moving too hurriedly or that we have just blown a fuse and it is time to consolidate.

Resistance is a sign that a change is trying to emerge from the unconscious. We sense it coming, but we may be afraid to make this life change. Perhaps it is an addiction or habit we don't want to let go of. Feelings of being overwhelmed often lead to resistance.

True resistance sometimes brings pain, but that is how we get moving. Without pain, some of us would never move. Through the painful experiences of the lower self, we gain the force necessary to die to ourselves and make room for higher consciousness.

Relapse and Fear

Relapse is a common problem. It usually happens to those who have not surrendered. With relapse, we have a tendency to blame ourselves, to think we are failures. This sets up an expectation of failure for the future. We think less of ourselves, so we relapse. This strengthens the self-blame/guilt thoughtform.

Whatever you do, don't picture yourself drinking alcohol. This might create just the reality you don't want. If you should slip and see yourself drinking, mentally break the picture into pieces, scatter it, and say, "Cancel!" Don't strengthen the alcoholism thoughtform by dwelling on the fact that you are an alcoholic. You are not an alcoholic; you are a blessed soul and a person who needs to channel his or her energy in a different way.

After a relapse, it is important to analyze the feelings you had just before it occurred. Low self-esteem, guilt, and self-pity are warning signals that you may be in danger of relapse. Lack of support is also a serious problem. That is why in the beginning you must surround yourself with friends who are happy for you, who will praise you for your will power and determination. Even if you think AA is not for you, find some kind of personal support system. It may save your life.

Boundaries

Alcoholics all have boundary problems. Boundaries are limits that say, "This is what I will or won't do for you. This is how far I will go. This is what I won't tolerate."

Most of us have boundaries when we start a relationship. We set up expectations about what we will or will not tolerate from other people. Alcoholism laughs at limits and boundaries. Growing up in dysfunctional homes, most of us never learned how to set limits. The disease pushes our boundaries farther and farther back until we are tolerating and doing things we said we would never do. Or we may reverse this trend and become intolerant of even the most innocent human behavior.

Alcoholics need boundaries. We need to set limits on what we will do to and for other people. We need to set limits on what we will allow people to do to and for us. We need to tell people exactly what these boundaries are and stick to them. However, I am not advocating inflexibility. As we grow and change, we may want to change our boundaries, but first we have to know how to establish what they are.

People may get angry at you for setting boundaries because they can't use you anymore. Be firm. You will probably be tested on every boundary you set up. People may not take you seriously at first. Tell people what your boundaries are—quietly, peacefully, and assertively.

Boundaries are worth the effort it takes to set them. People will respect you more. Ultimately, boundaries will give you more time and energy. Ask yourself now, "What boundaries do I need to set?"

Honesty

Honesty—both self-honesty and honesty with others— is of paramount importance in a recovery program. We must have the courage to take a long, hard look at ourselves and our faults, as well as the role they played in our drinking (AA's fourth and fifth steps). We must be willing to face what we have been afraid of facing, our own shadowy self that we have rejected and perhaps hidden from others. It is necessary to do this in order to be whole.

Karma

An understanding of reincarnation and the law of karma was an aid to my sobriety and has also been an aid to many others. Karma means, literally, "cause and effect"—we create our own reality. Whatever happens to us is what we *choose* to have happen, either consciously or subconsciously. We are responsible for everything that we have been, are, and will be. Our future consists of our accumulated karma, indicating the trends we have created by our own choices. According to the esoteric point of view, we chose our family members, the countries of our birth, our genders, our religions, our main trials, and our astrological configurations. The reason we chose our present circumstances was to solve our problems and to grow and unfold as spirit beings.

It is not my objective to go into detail about karma now.

The point I wish to make is that we *chose* alcoholism. There is no blame in this and no reason to feel sorry for ourselves. We set up our own realities. As spirits we *chose* to have painful experiences because through them we could acquire wisdom.

After death we forget, but the unconscious experience is part of our memory bank and influences our behavior in the next lifetime. How often we hear someone say, "I wish I didn't have this illness—life is awful!" That person chose the illness as a spirit but did not retain the memory of having done so. I consider a karmic memory accurate if it makes enough sense to explain a specific situation in the present lifetime. Alcoholism speeds up karma in that it forces us to face up to our problems and solve them in a mature manner.

Harmlessness

We should all practice harmlessness in thought, word, and deed. This prevents the accumulation of more karma. Since karma is one of the main causes of disease, it is best to clear away as much of it as possible. According to the AA program, the most common cause of relapse is resentments. That is why it is important to develop harmlessness. As long as we harbor enmity in our hearts toward anyone, we can develop a resentment. Resentment, in turn, creates more fears.

Forgiveness

If you feel enmity toward anyone, sit quietly and state firmly and lovingly, "I forgive you totally and completely. I hold no enmity in my heart toward anyone. If there is anything in my unconscious now that resembles it, I cast it upon the indwelling Christ to be resolved." If you are still having a hard time forgiving that person, call upon your higher self to dissolve the feeling. Send the person love. This should be done for every person you have ever wronged or toward whom you have felt anger. Take your time with this;

and if you feel resentment building up again, release it as soon as you can.

I cannot emphasize enough the importance of the Observer Self Meditation. Whenever we become intolerant and unforgiving toward ourselves, we draw into our lives more enmity. It is better to forgive ourselves, because only then can we begin to build the kind of world we truly deserve.

To conquer an addiction, it is essential to develop the polar opposite of those negative qualities associated with the addiction. In the case of alcoholism, if feelings of futility and oppression were a problem, generate feelings of joyfulness and zest for life; in place of low self-esteem, generate a sense of identity, self-worth, and independence; and in the place of guilt or self-hatred, generate self-acceptance.

The Role of Opposites

Learning the role of opposites is a primary part of every recovery program. In fact, understanding pairs of opposites is the key to solving all problems—to achieving balance in life and opening the doors to higher knowledge. In reality, there are no true opposites; we merely express them this way to categorize truth. We learn things by experiencing their opposites.

Take the pride/humility split. This often causes conflicts in recovery programs, for if we go too far with humility, humbling ourselves in a disparaging way, we hurt ourselves. What we are seeking is a balance. Once the dualism is understood, it can be transcended by self-acceptance. Then the pride/humility dualism will no longer be a problem for us.

Acceptance

Acceptance, which is based on surrender, is the foundation of any recovery program. When we don't accept ourselves, we draw unaccepting people into our lives. Acceptance of self leads to acceptance of others. Through our meditations (especially the Observer Self Meditation) we learn to observe ourselves nonjudgmentally. In time this changes consciousness, which in turn stirs us toward self-acceptance. Acceptance means surrendering the need to control, judge, or manipulate life—this is the key to trans-formation.

Co-Dependence

It is believed by some, including psychotherapist Anne Wilson Schaef, that many alcoholics are untreated co-dependents. Typical of co-dependency is a lack of identity. Accepting the ideas of parents, schools, and society causes us to accept false images of ourselves. Adopting these false images causes us to lose our own identities. This lack of identity—always looking to an external source for status—makes it very difficult for us to spontaneously respond to our true selves.

Spontaneous reaction with our higher selves cannot occur if others are controlling us. Nor can it occur when we think we must control life around us in order to live. Neither of these methods brings about the right relation-ship with ourselves or with others. Using our energy to control others only robs energy from ourselves. Yet if we stand in the shadow of someone else, our souls stand in darkness, too. This dependence on people, circumstances, or events no matter how subtle, still prevents the soul from expressing itself.

However, as Chris Griscom points out, once we begin our journey of self-discovery and unfoldment, there is no going back:

> The intense expansion of the ecstatic moment is often followed by an abrupt snapping-shut of the "windows to the sky." The new self suddenly experiences a profound feeling of nakedness. Stripped of all the old identities, it utterly reverses itself by charging backwards into the

familiar, seductive darkness. This turn of events is met with approval and relief by those around us, who, after all, cannot continue to maintain their emotional patterns if we suddenly abandon our supportive roles in their movies. We, in turn, cling desperately to the illusion that we can "ungrow" ourselves back to what we were before.[23]

Relationship Addiction

Since the advent of Robin Norwood's bestseller, *Women Who Love Too Much*, the concept of relationship addiction has emerged. This concept is an important one in understanding alcoholism, as many alcoholics are also relationship addicts. Unless a recovering person addresses this problem, sobriety will be hard to maintain for long.

I once knew a woman who had this problem. To be without a relationship for any length of time was unthinkable. She never had enough time to heal or to get to know herself. Today she is drinking herself to death.

In her book, Norwood contends that every woman in our culture is actively encouraged to behave in most of the ways that are typical of a very sick relationship addict—that is, to make another person the focus of her thoughts and actions; to be preoccupied with controlling, changing, and improving that other person; and to go to any length to do so. She is encouraged to be self-sacrificing and a martyr, and to be far more in touch with that other person's thoughts, feelings, and needs than with her own. Our cultural attitudes toward these behaviors make it almost impossible to fully realize just how unhealthy they are.

According to Norwood, the following are characteristics of a relationship addict:

1. Typically, you come from a dysfunctional home in which your emotional needs were not met.
2. You feel drawn to men or women who are emotion-

ally unavailable to you, and you have hopes of changing them.

3. Terrified of being abandoned, you will do almost any thing to keep the relationship going.
4. Accustomed to a lack of real nurturing in personal relationships, you will do anything to please or to help the person you are involved with.
5. When things go wrong in the relationship, you shoulder more than 50 percent of the guilt, blame, and responsibility.
6. You have low self-esteem and feel that you do not deserve to be happy.
7. Because of a lack of emotional security, you feel you must control your man or woman and the relationship at all times.
8. You waste time dreaming of what the relationship could be rather than seeing it for what it is now.
9. You are addicted to your emotional partner and to emotional pain.
10. You may be addicted biochemically or emotionally to drugs, alcohol, or food (especially sweets).
11. You are attracted to chaotic interpersonal situations that are emotionally painful. You do not focus on yourself and your needs.
12. You have a tendency toward bouts of depression and feeling sorry for yourself.
13. You are not attracted to men or women who are kind, considerate, stable, and reliable. Such people are boring to you.

To fully discuss relationship addiction would require a book in itself. For more information, refer to *Women Who Love Too Much*.

Life of Service

A life of service is mandatory for the recovering alcoholic. When we are recipients of spiritual energies, we are asked to share these energies with others so that they, too, may benefit. AA has always stressed the importance of service. Spiritual gifts unshared can result in psychological problems or a reversion to the old "unspiritual" self.

Alcoholism is caused by a spiritual predicament. The problem is that we have forgotten who we are. We are all here living at this time to rediscover our true selves. Overcoming our addictions is a process of self-discovery, of getting more in touch with our thoughts and feelings and coming to terms with our inner selves.

Recovery from alcoholism is not a process of "reforming" ourselves or trying to live up to others' images of what we should be, but one of *transforming*—accepting ourselves for who we are while learning how to operate on a higher frequency where we feel more relaxed, self-confident, and complete. With new identities formed through meditation, we raise our vibrations and merge with new consciousness that forever transforms our addictions.

Appendix

Following are some exercises that will help in your recovery. To perform them you should be in a relaxed, meditative state (not a trance). Surround yourself with white light for protection. Do breathing exercises to help you relax. Use centering and grounding exercises for each technique (see chapter 8).

Coming to Terms with Your Past

Stand up straight, and center and ground yourself. Close your eyes and breathe deeply five or six times. See yourself in a rose-colored, egg-shaped bubble. About eighteen inches above your head is your higher self (the soul-star). Picture this higher self as a shining star pouring light and warmth into your being.

Now begin to reflect on an experience in your past. Pretend you are viewing it on a movie screen. See it without judgment. You made the best choice you could have made, given the options you had at that time. Ascertain what you have learned from this past experience and how you can relate it to the present. Deal with unreleased emotions. Your past has determined your present, and your present will determine your future—the past does not determine the future.

See if there is anything about yourself in the present that you would like to keep. Now picture yourself in the future, manifesting those qualities. See people responding to you positively, and see yourself manifesting the lifestyle you want.

Dissolving Resentments

Alcoholics must use some form of emotional release. Otherwise, nursing resentments can bring about a drinking relapse. To prevent this, try the following exercise.

1. Go into a deeply meditative state and ask your higher self for help in releasing your resentments.

2. See yourself in a large egg-shaped, rose-colored bubble. Feel its warmth and protection. See your higher self or soul-star hovering eighteen inches above your head. Feel its warmth and protection.

3. Some distance away from you, create another bubble of rose-colored light, and inside it place a person toward whom you feel resentment. Imagine this person as clearly as you can. Relive the scene that is causing the resentment. See the resentment rising to the surface.

4. Imagine the second bubble as a powerful magnet, drawing out of you all of the resentment. Call on your higher self for help in releasing it. Ask it to help you forgive and let go of the situation.

5. After you have released as much as you can, move the second bubble around you to draw out unconscious or forgotten resentments.

6. When you have released as much as you are able, move the second bubble in front of you. If the person inside it is still unchanged, shrink the person in the bubble. This will reduce the power he or she has over you.

7. See a ball of fire in your own bubble burning up all the resentment that is left.

8. Let go of the fire and see it transformed into white light.

Releasing Guilt

You may want to do this exercise two or three times for each person or a situation on your list.

1. Go into a deep state of relaxed consciousness. Ask your higher self for help in releasing the guilt.
2. Create a large, egg-shaped lavender bubble completely surrounding you. In it is lavender light.
3. Create another bubble outside yourself. Fill it with lavender light and in it place a person or situation you feel guilty about. See the situation in as much detail as possible, reliving the events and allowing the guilt feelings to surface.
4. Imagine the second bubble becoming a powerful magnet, drawing out all the guilt that has accumulated within you. Call on your higher self for help.
5. After you feel a release, move the second bubble around behind you to draw out unconscious guilt feelings that were repressed.
6. When you have released as much as you are able, move the second bubble in front of you. If the situation is still unchanged, shrink it in the bubble. This will reduce the power it has over you.
7. See a ball of fire in your own bubble burning up the rest of the guilt. Ask your higher self's help in releasing the guilt, and ask for clarification on whether there is a need for making amends.
8. Let go of the lavender fire and see it transformed into white light.
9. Looking at the situation once again, call on the higher self for help in forgiving yourself. Once again picture yourself going through the scene. See what motivated you at that time, how you felt, how others were reacting to you. Understand that with the knowledge you have now, you would have chosen differently, but with the knowledge you had then, it was the best possible choice. Forgive yourself. See

yourself standing there being showered with white rain that cleanses you of all your guilt, and see the stream of rain carry the guilt out of the bubble.

Letting Go

There are times when we find it difficult to let go of a person or a situation. Here is an exercise that will help:

1. Go into a meditative state and connect with your higher self, expressing the desire to become detached from the person or situation.
2. Imagine that you are standing on the bank of a large river with a strong current. Picture a small boat tied there, carrying the person you want to be free of. There is a strong current tugging at the boat, ready to take it downstream.
3. Imagine the other person in as much detail as possible. Realize that he or she has a higher self, too, and that you wish to connect with his or her higher self to impress upon the person that you need to be free of the negative bond between the two of you.
4. Now pick up a big, sharp knife and use it to cut through the rope that ties the boat to the dock. Hold on to your end of the rope.
5. Hold the rope in your hand and say to the other person's higher self, "I release you. I have no hold on you, nor you on me. I release you to your own good."
6. Let go of the rope and watch as the current sweeps the other person downstream. Know that the river can't reverse the boat once it has gone downstream; it is gone for good.
7. Mourn if you feel the need, but know that better things are coming in to replace the grief.

Observer Self Meditation

Use this exercise whenever you are emotionally stuck in a situation or when you want to get outside your emotional reaction to a situation and see it from a wider perspective. To begin with, you may want to put on some quiet, meditative music.

Close your eyes and view yourself totally involved in the situation in which the problem is occurring. Relax. Be aware of what you are feeling as you view a particular scene in the situation. Notice your body movements. Notice how you appear to others and how they are reacting to you. What kind of energy is there and how is it affecting you? It is important to feel the essence of that experience. What are your intentions?

Now go back to the scene and pretend you have left your body and are watching from above. Watching from this angle, see the entire scene again. Notice how others are reacting to you. Notice the context of the situation, the place, the country where it is happening. What is the relevance of this particular time in history, this culture, this age?

Now very slowly descend back into your body and begin to act out the entire scene again, based on what you saw from above. Notice any changes you are making and how you are handling the situation. Be aware of how others are acting toward you. Are there changes on their part? How does your body look and feel? What additional insights are you deriving from the situation? Be aware of the needs of others and what is motivating their behavior, and notice your reactions to them now that you have this new awareness.

End the scene in whatever way feels comfortable for you.

Boundary Meditation

Use this exercise to dispel the negativity and judgments of others and to define the boundaries of their influence upon you.

> Go into a state of deep relaxation. Imagine yourself sitting in a bubble of white light. This white light represents your spiritual being and the positive thoughtforms with which you have surrounded yourself, and this light is helping you to combat your addiction. While sitting in the white bubble, become aware of a gray cloud surrounding you from the outside of the bubble. This gray cloud represents the negativity of other people. It might be the thoughts they are having about you or their negative words and emotions. See clearly that it is their negativity. Then draw the light from your higher self into the bubble and allow it to come out through the gray cloud. See the white light dispersing the gray cloud and all the negativity.

Look into the past for ways in which people's negative comments or predictions might still be influencing you. (For example, your father's comment that, "You're a loser—you'll never amount to anything.") Use this technique on all such potent material from the past that you feel is still affecting you adversely.

Notes

1. Satprem, *Sri Aurobindo or the Adventure of Consciousness* (New York: Institute for Evolutionary Research, 1984), p. 253.
2. Ibid., p. 254.
3. Alice Bailey, *Esoteric Healing* (New York: Lucis Trust Publishing, 1951), p. 24.
4. Robert G. Bell, *Escape from Addiction* (New York: McGraw-Hill, 1970).
5. Bailey, *Esoteric Healing,* p. 15.
6. John Randolph Price, *The Planetary Commission* (Texas: Quartus Foundation for Spiritual Research, 1984), p. 112.
7. Anne Wilson Schaef, *Co-Dependence: Misunderstood, Mistreated* (San Francisco: Harper & Row, 1986), p. 34.
8. D.L. Gerard, G. Saenger, and R. Wile, "The Abstinent Alcoholic," Archives of General Psychiatry (1982), pp. 99-111.
9. Abraham Maslow, *Toward a Psychology of Being* (New York: Van Nostrand Reinhold, 1986), p. 26.
10. Milton Bullock, "Stay Drugfree Naturally," *East West: The Journal of Natural Health & Healing* (March 1988), p. 41.
11. *Twelve Steps and Twelve Traditions* (New York: AA World Services, Inc., 1979), pp. 5-13.
12. Women for Sobriety (Quakertown, PA: 1951), p. 29.
13. Lucille Cedercrans, *The Nature of the Soul* (Privately published, 1957), p. 53.
14. Ibid., p. 73.

15. Hal Stone and Sidra Winkelman, from John Bradshaw, *Healing the Shame that Binds You* (Deerfield Beach, FL: 1988), p. 143.
16. Roberto Assagioli, *Psychosynthesis* (New York: Penguin Books, 1979), p. 44.
17. Edith Fiore, *The Unquiet Dead: A Psychologist Treats Spirit Possession* (New York: Ballantine Books, 1978), p. 119.
18. Gopi Krishna, *Kundalini: The Evolutionary Energy in Man* (Boston: Shambhala Publications), p. 13.
19. Chris Griscom, *Ecstasy Is a New Frequency* (Santa Fe, NM: Bear & Company, 1987), p. 60.
20. Two Disciples, *The Rainbow Bridge* (Escondido, CA: The Triune Foundation, 1981).
21. Mabel Collins, *Through the Gates of Gold* (Pasadena, CA: Theosophical University Press, 1976), pp. 69, 72.
22. Griscom, *Ecstasy Is a New Frequency*, p. 21.
23. Ibid., p. 171.

Glossary

ACCULTURATION: The process of acquiring the cultural traditions of a society. Socialization.

AJNA CHAKRA: The spiritual center located between the eyebrows, also known as the third eye.

ASTRAL BODY: An energy body extending out from the physical body and comprised of the emotions and the auric field.

ASTRAL DIMENSION: A level of energy more refined than physical matter, influenced by the thoughts and emotions of humanity.

ASTRAL PLANE: The plane on which the emotions of humanity register collectively.

ASTRAL POLLUTION: Unwanted energies or entities in the auric field.

ASTRAL STATE: Being out of body and existing in the astral dimension.

AURA: A natural emanation of energy given out by a living being. The electromagnetic field surrounding all living things. This force field may be seen psychically as a fluid, pulsating, oval-shaped ring of light, or it may appear as a swirling pattern of light with several colors shimmering through it.

AUTONOMY: Independence, self-regulation.

CARTESIAN: Referring to the philosophy of mathematician-philosopher Rene Descartes.

CENTERING: The act of calming one's own nervous system; going deep within one's consciousness in order to reach a sense of equilibrium.

CHAKRA: One of the seven major energy centers located at various points from the base of the spine to the crown of the head. Each chakra governs a different aspect of life, and all of the human energy bodies or levels of consciousness are joined at these points.

CLAIRAUDIENCE: The ability to psychically hear what lies beyond physical sound.

CLAIRVOYANCE: The ability to psychically see what lies beyond normal sight.

CONSCIOUSNESS: The total collection of one's thoughts, feelings, and beliefs molded into a structure of awareness, understanding, and knowledge of both the visible and invisible worlds.

CRYSTALLIZED: Fixed and definite in form.

DELIRIUM TREMENS: A very serious withdrawal state. The symptoms of delirium tremens include severe tremors, agitation, fast pulse, and intense disorientation.

DISCARNATE ENTITY: A spirit that is trapped in the physical world without its physical body.

DISIDENTIFICATION: The realization that one is not one's emotions, physical body, or mental states; that these aspects are parts of the self but not the central "I," the essence.

DUALISM: The perception of reality as two principles instead of one. Dualism is caused by the limitations of human intelligence and by modern American culture, which fosters this mode of thinking. Dualism disappears in *samadhi*, in which both the intellect and senses are transcended.

DWELLER ON THE THRESHOLD: The sum total of one's negative tendencies as expressed through the personality.

EARTHBOUND ENTITY: A spirit that remains in the physical world after death because it has not made a successful transition into the higher realms. According to esoteric theory, an earthbound entity is actually trapped in the lower realms.

ECSTASY: Spontaneous cosmic attunement occurring in deep meditation, prayer, and other spiritual activities that lifts one far beyond the realm of the physically normal.

EMOTIONAL BODY: The body of consciousness or entity

comprised of feelings and emotions, which vibrates at a very low frequency.

ENTITY: A living being possessing a soul.

ESOTERIC: That which pertains to metaphysical concepts.

ETHERIC BODY: The envelope of the soul.

EXPANSION OF CONSCIOUSNESS: A growth and expansion of awareness.

EXORCIST: A highly trained specialist who uses force to expel discarnate spirits from those who are possessed.

FALSE PERSONALITY: The personality that consists of what one thinks of oneself based on the perceptions of others and one's role in society.

FREE FLOWING: Not holding onto one's schedule or expectations in the face of changes.

GROUNDING: Creation of a secure attachment and connection with the Earth. Grounding permits the energy from the Earth to flow through the soles of the feet and into the body. If one is not "grounded," one feels nervous or "spaced out," is hyperactive, and is often less effective in daily life. Alcoholics have an especially hard time staying grounded.

HATHA YOGA: A system of yoga in which the various parts of the body are used to effect the control of the mind through an elaborate system of *asanas*, or postures. These *asanas* are useful for maintaining physical health as well as for spiritual progress.

HIGHER SELF: The ideal self, the greater consciousness that has always existed. Also known as the "voice of the soul."

INTEGRATION: The organization of the components of self (essence and personality) into a coordinated, harmonious whole.

KARMIC BLUEPRINT: The blueprint of the soul for erasing all karmic obligations.

KUNDALINI FIRE: The life force of the universe, the Christ consciousness, the supreme potential of humanity, the feminine creative force of the universe.

LAW OF KARMIC BALANCING: The idea that if we do

something good, it will come back to us, and that if we harm someone, this will also return to us.

LOWER SELF: The lesser self or human self that is identified primarily with the emotions, the personality, and physical survival; the ego.

MANTRA: A sacred word or cosmic sound invested with the power of God, the repetition of which is intended to bring about a shift in consciousness.

MASS MIND: The collective mind of humanity.

MEDITATION: The conscious act of stilling the mind by stopping the flow of images and thoughts. It is often done with the use of a mantra.

MEDIUMSHIP: Allowing a spirit from the higher planes to manifest through one's body—most commonly by speaking, writing, painting, and even while healing others.

MENTAL BODY: The vehicle of consciousness or entity comprised of thoughts, ideas, mental processes, creativity, and so forth.

MULTIDIMENSIONALITY: The state of existing or being aware of more than one dimension at the same time.

NADIS: Channels through which the life force is circulated throughout the human body.

OUIJA BOARD: A board printed with the letters of the alphabet, "yes," "no," and numbers, plus a planchette that moves on the board to spell out messages. It is used for contacting spirits.

PARTIAL SELF: A fragment of the personality that is not directed by the higher self.

PAST-LIFE THERAPY: Psychotherapy that involves regressions to former lifetimes in order to solve current problems.

PHYSICAL BODY: The physical form of consciousness existing as part of third-dimensional matter. It is the most dense of the four bodies.

POLTERGEIST: A "noisy" ghost, usually a manifestation of an uncontrolled energy that may cause knocking sounds, hurled or transported objects, and phenomena involving water and fire. These things are frequently caused by the subconscious energies of a human being presently living.

POSSESSION: See "spirit obsession."

PRANA: The life breath, the vital force of the body and universe that sustains life and is the power of animation.

PSYCHIC: A person who is sensitive to perceptions other than those received through the five physical senses.

PSYCHIC ATTACK: An instance in which one becomes opposed by a force, energy, or intelligence either not on his or her particular wavelength or actually "anti" the frequency of his or her energy. Whenever one is immersed in the astral dimension, psychic attack becomes possible.

PSYCHIC DEVELOPMENT: The conscious effort to develop abilities such as clairvoyance, mediumship, clairaudience, and so forth.

RAJA YOGA: The yoga of eight steps directed toward the purification and control of the mind.

RECIDIVISM: A relapse into the disease of alcoholism after one has attained temporary sobriety.

REPRESSION: A defense mechanism of the mind in which there is a "forgetting" of an experience that is emotionally or physically painful.

SACRAL CENTER: The second chakra, located between the ovaries for women and an inch or so below the navel for men. It has to do with reproduction and sexuality.

SAMADHI: A transcendental state of awareness in which one experiences the supreme reality and becomes self-realized. This state occurs when the topmost chakra is fully activated.

SELF-ACTUALIZED: Completely realized in one's own individuality; having a fullness of experience.

SENSITIVE: As an adjective: Having acute physical or mental perceptions, or emotional sensibility. As a noun: A person usually susceptible and aware of psychic influences.

SOLAR PLEXUS CHAKRA: A concentrated center of energy in the area of the stomach and liver that looks like a whirling wheel or a flower with ten petals. It is associated with power issues.

SPEEDING UP OF KARMA: Karmic obligations falling away at a faster pace due to the speeding up of one's personal evolution.

SPIRIT OBSESSION: The act of a discarnate entity from the lower planes psychically transferring his or her feelings, desires, hangups, or thoughts to a presently incarnated person. The transference often occurs so gradually that it goes unnoticed.

SPIRITUAL BODY: The vehicle of consciousness that is the essence or soul.

STEREOTYPE: An oversimplified, widely held, and often erroneous belief.

SUBCONSCIOUS MIND: The region of the mind containing forgotten and repressed material relating to a person's life.

SUBTLE ENERGY: Electromagnetic energy moving slowly up the spine.

VIBRATION: Emanations of energy given off from the fields of invisible energy surrounding every living thing.

VICTIM CONSCIOUSNESS: The false belief that one is at the mercy of events beyond one's control. The refusal to admit that one's life is the result of a series of personal choices.

VORTEX: A place on Earth that responds to galactic energy.

YOGA: A state of oneness with the self, or the practices and spiritual disciplines leading to that state.

Bibliography

Abrahamson, E.M. *Body, Mind, and Sugar*. New York: Avon Books, 1977.

Assagioli, Roberto. *Psychosynthesis*. New York: Penguin Books, 1979.

Bailey, Alice. *Esoteric Psychology*. Vols. 1, 2. New York: Lucis Publishing Co., 1962.

_____. *Esoteric Healing*. New York: Lucis Publishing Co., 1951.

Bass, Ellen, and Laura Davis. *The Courage to Heal: A Guide for Women—Survivors of Child Sexual Abuse*. New York: Harper & Row, 1988.

Bradshaw, John. *Healing the Shame that Binds You*. Deerfield Beach, FL: Health Communications, 1988.

Cedercrans, Lucille. *The Nature of the Soul*. Privately published, 1957.

Chia, Mantak. *Awakening Healing Energy Through the Tao*. Santa Fe, NM: Aurora Press, 1983.

Clow, Barbara Hand. *Eye of the Centaur*. Santa Fe, NM: Bear & Company, 1989.

_____. *Heart of the Christos: Starseeding from the Pleiades*. Santa Fe, NM: Bear & Company, 1989.

_____. *Chiron: Rainbow Bridge Between the Inner and Outer Planets*. St. Paul, MN: Llewellyn Publications, 1987.

Collins, Mabel. *Through the Gates of Gold*. Pasadena, CA: Theosophical University Press, 1976.

Cunningham, Scott. *The Magic of Incense, Oils, and Brews: A Guide to Their Preparation and Use*. St. Paul: Llewellyn Publications, 1986.

DeRohan, Ceanne. *Right Use of Will: Healing and Evolving the Emotional Body.* Santa Fe, NM: Four Winds Publications, 1986.

Dufty, William. *Sugar Blues.* New York: Warner Books, 1976.

Ferguson, Marilyn. *The Aquarian Conspiracy: Personal and Social Transformation in the Eighties.* Los Angeles: Jeremy P. Tarcher Inc., 1980.

Fiore, Edith. *The Unquiet Dead: A Psychologist Treats Spirit Possession.* New York: Ballantine Books, 1987.

Fortune, Dion. *Psychic Self-Defense.* London: Society of the Inner Light, 1930.

Green, Jeff. *Uranus: Freedom From the Known.* St. Paul: Llewellyn Publications, 1988.

Griscom, Chris. *Ecstasy Is a New Frequency.* Santa Fe, NM: Bear & Company, 1987.

Grof, Stanislav and Christina. *Spiritual Emergency: When Personal Transformation Becomes a Crisis.* Los Angeles: Jeremy P. Tarcher Inc., 1989.

Haich, Elisabeth, and Selvarajan Yesudian. *Self Healing, Yoga and Destiny.* Santa Fe, NM: Aurora Press, 1983.

Judith, Anodea. *The Wheels of Life: A User's Guide to the Chakra System.* St. Paul: Llewellyn Publications, 1987.

Krishna, Gopi. *Kundalini: The Evolutionary Energy in Man.* Boston: Shambhala Publications, 1967.

Maslow, Abraham H. *Toward a Psychology of Being.* 2d ed. New York: Van Nostrand Reinhold & Co., 1968.

Merchant, Carolyn. *The Death of Nature: Women's Ecology and Scientific Evolution.* New York: Harper & Row, 1983.

Myers, Judy: *Staying Sober: A Nutrition and Exercise Program for the Recovering Alcoholic.* New York: Congdon & Weed, Inc., 1983.

Norwood, Robin. *Women Who Love Too Much.* New York: St. Martin's Press, 1985.

Phelps, Janice K., and Alan E. Nourse. *The Hidden Addiction and How to Get Free.* Boston: Little, Brown & Co., 1986.

Pollard, III, John K. *Self Parenting: The Complete Guide to Your Inner Conversations.* Malibu, CA: Generic Human Studies Publishing, 1987.

Price, John R. *The Planetary Commission.* Austin, TX: Quartus Foundation for Spiritual Research, 1984.

Royce, James E., *Alcoholism Problems and Alcohol.* New York: The Free Press, 1981.

Sannella, Lee, M.D. *The Kundalini Experience: Psychoses or Transcendence.* Lower Lake, CA: Integral Publishing, 1987.

Satprem. *Sri Aurobindo or the Adventure of Consciousness.* New York: Institute for Evolutionary Research, 1984.

Schaef, Anne Wilson. *When Society Becomes an Addict.* San Francisco: Harper & Row, 1987.

_____. *Co-Dependence: Misunderstood, Mistreated.* San Francisco: Harper & Row, 1986.

Sinetar, Marsha. *Ordinary People as Monks and Mystics: Lifestyles for Self-Discovery.* New York: St. Paul Press, 1986.

Steiner, Claude M. *Healing Alcoholism.* New York: Grove Press, 1975.

Two Disciples. *The Rainbow Bridge.* Escondido, CA: The Triune Foundation, 1981.

Whitfield, Charles I. *Healing the Child Within.* Pompano Beach, FL: Health Communications, 1987.

About the Author

Joyce Bismack was raised in Milford, Connecticut, graduating from Southern Connecticut State University with a Bachelor of Arts degree in psychology. For the past twenty years she has worked as a bookstore owner, a chemical abuse counselor, and a paralegal, studying metaphysics throughout this time.

A powerful mystical experience and spiritual awakening at the age of twenty-two launched her into many years of emotional turmoil, later identified as manifestations of a kundalini awakening. This process has led her through much soul searching and study. Her particular area of interest is the relationship between mysticism and chemical addiction. She believes that most alcoholics are mystics and muses of the soul—creative people who have a gift for the passionate life, yet who have been societal misfits most of their lives.

Bismack has become aware that present-day alcoholic recovery programs are not as successful as they could be. She feels that what is needed is a holistic program that takes into consideration all the elements of recovery: emotional, physical, mental, and spiritual. She is currently working on a book on co-dependence.

Books of Related Interest
by Bear & Company

BREATHING
Expanding Your Power and Energy
by Michael Sky

DANCING WITH THE FIRE
Transforming Limitation Through Firewalking
by Michael Sky

ECSTASY IS A NEW FREQUENCY
Teachings of The Light Institute
by Chris Griscom

EMERGENCE OF THE DIVINE CHILD
Healing the Emotional Body
by Rick Phillips

EYE OF THE CENTAUR
A Visionary Guide into Past Lives
by Barbara Hand Clow

HEART OF THE CHRISTOS
Starseeding from the Pleiades
by Barbara Hand Clow

LIGHT: MEDICINE OF THE FUTURE
How We Can Use It to Heal Ourselves NOW
by Jacob Liberman, O.D., Ph.D.

Contact your local bookseller or write:
BEAR & COMPANY
P.O. Drawer 2860
Santa Fe, NM 87504